BY THE S[illegible]

Couples Arguing (Darton, Longman & Todd, 1987).

Couples in Counselling (Darton, Longman & Todd, 1989).

Couples Growing (Darton, Longman & Todd, 1991).

Couples Parting (Darton, Longman & Todd, 1992).

Don't Blame Me! (Sheldon Press, 1990).

The Care Guide (Cassell, 1995, ed. Michael Jacobs) Contributor.

CONTENTS

PREFACE

On being asked what was most difficult to man, the Greek Philosopher Thales answered: "To know one's self."

In almost every aspect of our lives, 'change' seems to be the order of the day. Daily, we are bombarded through a highly organised advertising industry to change our cars, our computers, our homes – so that we remain 'up-to-date'. Our TV screens are full of programmes about 'change' – for example *Changing Rooms*. 'Makeovers' are there to keep us from settling for 'yesterday's colours'; even our gardens are not excluded from this clamour for alteration. Significantly, the concept of changing human personality is omitted from the list. Mind you, the implications are there in abundance. If you use product 'X', or wear designer 'Y' clothing you will find your lives transformed! Rubbish, of course. The cynics turn away from their TV screens saying, 'You can't change human nature'. And that's rubbish, too!

There seems to be an assumption that people are – well, just people: fixed, predictable, permanent. We know who we are, don't we? What you see is what you get. Aren't we all just victims of our genetic make-up, our DNA, our upbringing, our culture? And you can't change the past, can you? It will be the purpose of this book to challenge some of these assumptions.

I have noticed, during a lifetime of exercising pastoral and psychotherapeutic care, that whenever I ask someone the question, "Who are you?" (although it is usually wrapped in a more friendly way, such as, "Tell me about yourself"), I invariably receive a reply concerning their job, what they *do*. *Being* and *doing*, who I am and what I do, are somehow confused in most people's minds.

"Who are you?"
"I'm Sid, the Plumber".
"But who are you, Sid?"
"Er..."

Sid appears stumped. As if I've asked him a question straight out of University Challenge on the theory of Quantum mechanics.

Sid is not alone. Most of us hesitate when confronted by this question, which is why it is so seldom asked. I remember a line from an old Goon Show script, when Eccles was being questioned by the police:

Policeman: "What's your name?"
Eccles: "Ah, the tricky ones first, eh?"

We don't want to embarrass people by asking 'tricky questions'. So we sidestep the question and settle for a description of what work they do, how they employ their time, their level of productivity. Answers along the line of, "I'm a plumber" or "I'm retired" actually avoid the question: they do not answer it. Strangely, people like Sid above, often think that they *have* answered the question, "Who are you?"

I recall one of the students in a Counselling workshop and asking who she was. She replied, "I'm a Vicar's wife". I contradicted this by saying, "No, you're not!" I reminded her that I did not ask about her *role*, or what she did, but who she was. She grew angry and maintained fiercely that she *was* a Vicar's wife. I disagreed, and asked why she defined herself by her work, by her *relationship* to her husband, instead of her Self. I said I was not interested in what she did, but how she defined herself. What could she tell me about her Self? She was not alone in having difficulty even understanding my question.

Of course, we have only ourselves to blame for this confusion. When other people meet us for the first time and ask who we are, they usually *mean*, 'Where do you fit in with the scheme of things?" Giving them answers about plumbing or being married to a Vicar are precisely what they wish to know. They do not want to know about our personality, our selfhood, our uniqueness, our aspirations, our feelings.

A number of reasons may be found for this strange reluctance to tell other people who we are, but the most basic reason is this: we simply don't know ourselves! I mean, we simply do not know our *Selves*. Most of us have not a clue who we are in the innermost core of our being. And if we *do* have a clue, then it is probably something shameful that must be hidden at all costs. Mustn't let people see what we're really like!

So the title of this book, *Who do you think you are?* is not a superfluous question. It drives to the heart of our individuality and our uniqueness as persons. And the guarantee I will make is this: *You are **not** who you think you are.* I realise that this is fighting talk, and that you are entitled to ask me to put my money where my mouth is!

Should we be asked, say, at a party, "Who are you?", we are entitled to give the answer that lies behind the question. Other people do not expect a run down on our cultural, sexual, emotional characteristics that go to make up who we are; they are not interested in a summary of what makes us unique. They usually want to know *what we do*. Like most other people, I too play the game and may answer, "A psychotherapist", or "A writer" or whichever of my *personae* seems appropriate. If I choose to be pedantic I may reply, "I'm Tony". Social gatherings have their own set of expectations, but baring your soul is not usually one of them.

The relative pronouns 'Who' and 'What' often get mixed up in general conversation, as do the verbs 'doing' and 'being', and in some cases they are regarded as interchangeable. I accept, of course, that while strictly speaking for Sid to say, "I am a plumber" is incorrect – he was not born a plumber, plumbing is not about his essence, he is merely *employed* as one - we will go along with this in the context of getting our leaking pipes seen to. Plumbing is about this man's doing, not his being. I do not suggest in this case the answer should be, "I plumb!" Although, "I mend broken pipes" is a perfectly sensible answer.

But the implications of this interchangeable use of language is important when it comes to defining who a person is in their individual uniqueness. Such sloppy use of language leads to people not only defining themselves in terms of their work, but also, more importantly, *their only sense of worth is through their employment.* They are only as good as they *do.* The dangers of this state of affairs is obvious.

If we have imbued our *productivity* with the sum of our feelings of worth and self-esteem, then we are a psychological accident looking for somewhere to happen! Look what happens when we don't or can't work – what then? What happens when we are ill or retire from work? Quite apart from the financial implications to these states of affairs there are very strong psychological implications too.

Having no *work*, we believe that we have no *worth.*

That is precisely how I felt queuing up at the local dole office; having no work I felt my self-esteem drop to almost zero.

I had no role other than 'unemployed' – and it felt lousy. It added significantly to my depression.

We don't usually speak about this, but this is often what we are feeling deep down inside ourselves. Indeed, we may have no words to express what we are feeling; we simply let our bodies do the speaking for us. We slide into depression.

Having hung our sense of worth and self-esteem around the hook of our working lives, we have made ourselves a hostage to fortune. We become a time-bomb just waiting to explode.

Popular thinking says that in order to increase our sense of self-worth we must climb the corporate ladder; we are only as good as we do, and by promotion we gain a higher slot in the 'feel-good' stakes. Such advancement is seen in the status symbols with which we surround ourselves: our cars, our houses, our clothing, our holiday destinations and even where our children go to school.

There is no suggestion here that ambition is wrong or that by aiming for the top in our work or profession is unworthy. The point I will make in this book is that these perfectly laudable aims often serve as *substitutes* for self-belief; never mind the quality, feel the width! If I look good, I must *be* good. While this outer armour may work for a while, there are going to be times when our camouflage fails; we begin to feel that deep down inside us is a feeling of dissatisfaction. Something's wrong.

I recall visiting a parishioner in the "millionaires' row" of my parish. The Jaguar was in the yard, the gardener was clearing leaves from the swimming pool, the house was enormous. Inside, the whole décor and furnishings reeked of opulence. The maid invited me upstairs to the lady of the house who was confined to bed. I gawped at the wall-to-wall wardrobes packed out with Paris models, and couldn't help comparing it with our rather Spartan surroundings in the Vicarage! During our conversation, the lady sat up and waved her hand around in mid-air. "You see all this?" she asked. "It's just a shell!"

She had surrounded herself with luxury with a capital 'L' – there was no status symbol missing, yet it had all suddenly collapsed as a means of keeping at bay a gnawing unhappiness and a suicidal depression. She certainly knew what she possessed – but she had no inkling of who she was. Suddenly one day, she spotted the flaw in her life: there was something inside her that was crying to come out and that something was pain. She'd tried everything money could buy to keep that voice at bay but she had now run out of ideas. Maybe the Vicar had an answer.

There was nothing wrong with the materialism that comprised this woman's life. There was nothing wrong with her life-style. She was perfectly entitled to fly off to Paris for some weekend shopping. But what was wrong lay in the fact that it was unbalanced; her life was all on the outside: it was 'just a shell'. Her life-style was a substitute for an inner craving that nothing external could either reach or satisfy. It was like deciding to have the house repainted when the kitchen was on fire.

This lady is not alone. In many ways she could be seen as a typical, if sad, example of much that comprises modern living. We seem to have settled for the confusion of identifying ourselves by our possessions or bank balance or status, rather than in our personal self-esteem. How did this evidence present itself to me? It's a fair question.

In my early days of pastoral ministry, back in the 1960's, I believed that the answer was God. Such people lacked a spiritual dimension to their materialistic lives, and if they would only turn to Him their problems would be answered.

And in a surprising number of instances it proved to be so. I noticed how some people's lives were changed as they underwent a painful reappraisal of their system of values and made a re-alignment of their lives according to moral and spiritual concerns. They certainly assured me that they felt much happier for doing so.

But this was not so for many other people to whom I ministered. The 'God-package' in which such changes were wrapped up appeared quite unacceptable to a number of people. This was partly my fault - maybe more a short-sightedness on my part. I was merely passing on to others the 'way' which had worked in my own life. To be sure, I had experienced a change in my life through an evangelical conversion during my National Service in the Royal Air Force. It would be many years later that I would discover how even such a spiritual experience had left many questions unanswered and issues un-addressed. Indeed, to a certain extent, this experience became a further cloak to my real inner needs.

The unquestionable acceptance by God that I discovered in handing my life over to Him would eventually be seen as a subtle form of substitution for acceptance by my *Self*. In spite of my conversion, my inner neurosis remained intact; having come to the light, much of my inner world remained in darkness. My core pain and interior defence system remained untouched. Whatever vague symptoms did emerge from my inner core (anxiety, dreams, sexual fantasies) were discharged into an increasingly long prayer list. But nothing stopped the nagging sense that all was not well within, in spite of a whole arsenal of spiritual exercises. In spite of all the external evidence of 'success' in my vocation there was a large part of me outside of my conscious awareness.

It took my entrance into a Mid-life Transition to bring my

elaborate system of subterfuge crashing down about my head. John Milton in his *Paradise Lost* described it as follows:

Which way shall I fly
Infinite wrath and infinite despair?
Which way I fly is hell; myself am hell;
And in the lowest deep a lower deep,
Still threat'ning to devour me, opens wide,
To which the hell I suffer seems a heaven.

Many years later I would discover the characteristics of the Mid-life Transition (popularly called a *Mid-Life Crisis*) particularly in Daniel Levinson's helpful book [1978]*. How accurate they proved to be in my own experience.

Levinson explains:

> *But for the great majority of men...this period evokes tumultuous struggles within the self and with the external world...They cannot go on as before, but need time to choose a new path or modify the old one. A profound reappraisal of this kind cannot be a cool, intellectual process. It must involve emotional turmoil, despair, the sense of not knowing where to turn or of being stagnant and unable to move at all.* [p.199]

Together with our own inner hesitations, however, such struggles do not go unopposed from external sources.

* Books are referred to by their date of publication and will be found in the Bibliography on p.169f.

> *He will often be opposed by other persons and institutions – his wife, children, boss, parents, colleagues, the occupational system in which he works, the implicit web of social conformity – that seem to maintain order and prevent change.* [p.200]

The climax of our metamorphosis may either come when, through therapy, we make a conscious choice to undergo a painful inner exploration of depths hitherto unrecognised or denied, or – in cases where the choice is simply taken out of our hands – we experience a mental breakdown. Either way the issues remain the same:

> *In the Mid-life Transition, these neglected parts of the self urgently seek expression. A man experiences them as 'other voices in other rooms' (in Truman Capote's evocative phrase). Internal voices that have been muted for years now clamour to be heard. At times they are heard as a vague whispering, the content unclear but the tone indicating grief over lost opportunities, outrage over betrayal by others, or guilt over betrayal by oneself... A man hears the voice of an identity prematurely rejected... During the Mid-life transition he must learn to listen more attentively to these voices and decide consciously what part he will give them in his life. [ibid.]*

During the course of my own time in psychotherapy I experienced what can only be described as a total re-orientation of my life. It involved a full exploration of the 'cellar' of my life, that area of my psyche in which I had placed – or had had placed for me – the darker side of my life, what Jung would call my Shadow. As a result I discovered my Self, that part of me I had been hiding from and denying (albeit unconsciously) for most of my life.

I share this process with you quite openly at the beginning of what for some of you may be a similar journey into wholeness and happiness. I am not proposing anything I have not been through myself, even though my contours and issues may be quite different from yours. It is time for radical change, not merely adding another Band-Aid to the many we have already tried.

In this book I will try and address the major issues to be faced in the journey into self-discovery and personal transformation.

We shall start from our cellular beginnings, from our very genetic make-up and external circumstances that formed us *in utero* – a subject that even today is still fraught with controversy, yet proving to be crucial in our understanding of our developing selfhood. Moving on from our intra-uterine influences we reach the family surroundings into which we were born, and where we learned, in our most vulnerable state, the rules of the world. Needing to find some way to protect ourselves, we shall then study the intricate network of human defences which we adopted in order to survive. Such defences are not without cost, however, and in Chapter four we shall see the outcome in the masks we wear in the world.

Chapter five is when we begin to clear out the 'wardrobe' that other people have supplied for our identity, and decide to choose one that more accurately displays who we really are. Chapter six deals with the important battle between our autonomy and the authority of others, and the thorny accusation of 'being selfish'. Finally, we find ways to declare and celebrate our new-found Self.

This work does not pretend to be definitive. As its subtitle suggests, it is but an *introduction* to self-discovery.

If it helps you to decide to make this journey into life for yourself, to want to discover who you *really* are, to recover a sense of your personal worth and self-esteem, then it would have met my hopes and aspirations.

CHAPTER ONE
Theme: Derivation

HOW DID I BECOME ME?

"When did 'I' begin?
When do 'I' end?
What am I?
Am I?"
[R. D. Laing: 1976, p.19]

INTRODUCTION

This book addresses a question that at some point in our lives we are almost bound to ask, or others may ask of us. Perhaps its title may be thrown at us in the process of an argument ("Who do you think **you** are?") implying that we are somehow getting 'above our station'. It can come in the form of a challenge from someone who feels that we may be pushing ourselves forward or claiming too much for ourselves. The real problem lies, I believe, in the fact that most of us have never really asked *ourselves* this question, nor gone on to satisfy ourselves about the important issue of our identity. As Ronnie Laing asks, "What am I?"

There is something endemic within the British culture (as opposed, say, to that of the United States) that would both give – and expect – a *negative* reply to our question. People raised within our culture would almost inevitably give a list of their faults, shortcomings, sins even. None but the most casehardened personality would parade his or her merits and respond with a positive celebration of their worth. There are no prizes for guessing where this trait originates.

It seems that, somewhere along our developmental or evolutionary line, it has been become a *virtue* to think badly about ourselves. Or, at the very least, we certainly must not parade anything that may be taken for pride. Not giving our children 'big heads' has become a major objective for many parents. There is an obsession, and I put it as strongly as that, with ensuring that we play down any achievements or qualities other than with a heavy slice of discounting: "I passed the exam, *but only just*!" "Oh, it was pure luck!" "I didn't do as well as so-and-so!" (When I first felt the full culture shock of living in the United States – and even before that, just talking to American soldiers during the Second World War – they came across as incredibly self-assured, braggarts even. They were certainly un-British in their self-promotion!) The pattern for such British self-effacement is all too clear: in a word, *conditioning*.

In all sorts of ways, the ideas that humility is better than pride, self-depreciation is better than self-appreciation, self-denial is better than self-assertion, have entered our social psyche to such an extent that they have assumed the power and character of Divine Law. Even to challenge their rectitude is almost to take issue with God! So, we have been culturally conditioned to put others first, to think better of other people than we do of ourselves, to enhance the achievement of others while at the same deprecating our own.

What I will put forward in this book is not a total reversal of these ideas, so that we could end up proposing a society with a hard-nosed, "Me first!" mentality. Rather, a society in which we hold a balance between affirming the worth of others, *as well as* our own. Not to choose between them, but to hold both together. If you should think that this is reversing a genuine Divine Law, I would only remind you of the Second Commandment which says, "You shall love your neighbour *as yourself*." Alas, the last two words often get left out of the debate.

Therefore, I will be inviting you to take a journey with me in order to find out how you, as an individual, came to possess the knowledge about who you think you are. You will be in for a few shocks, of that I have no doubt. I may ask you to take some things on trust until my argument is concluded. In order to check your progress you may care to write down, now, five things by which you would identify yourself, or five characteristics you believe about yourself. You can then compare them with how you feel about yourself at the end of our journey.

One thing I will guarantee: wherever you start out in this enquiry into your personal identity you will end up somewhere else, and hopefully, *someone* else. So, as in all the best mythic stories, let us begin at the beginning.

MY BEGINNING

At what point in time did I start to become me? The issues surrounding the subject of Selfhood are, of course, vast and complex. They baffle the minds of the greatest researchers as they have done from time immemorial. One of the earliest pioneers in the field of human development was Sigmund Freud and he included the 'neonatal phase' as the earliest in his own system of 'phases of human development'. There was, unfortunately, no attempt on the part of Freud to give more than a passing acknowledgement to the important aspect of the life of the foetus *in utero.*

Some of the early followers of Freud were aware of this significant omission. In an important book, *The Trauma of Birth* (1924), Otto Rank, the Austrian psychoanalyst - who, at one time, was seen as Freud's 'heir-apparent' - traced the source of all future anxiety back to the trauma of the birth process. Although Freud acknowledged Rank's views as 'the most important progress since the discovery of psychoanalysis' he eventually parted company with Rank on this vital issue. Rank saw clearly that severe attacks of anxiety in adult life were possibly re-enactments of the original birth trauma. It was to be another fifty years before the full impact of this important theory was to be understood.

IS THE WOMB A ROOM WITH A VIEW?

But this was only a beginning. What of the nine months preceding birth? Could they possible have any relevance to our later development? Until recently, little attention has been given to the developing person *in utero.* From the medical perspective, it was the condition of the mother that was all-important. Indeed, until the invention of modern technology doctors had little knowledge (or interest?) in what the foetus was experiencing. Even so, such interest was merely physical: the all-important success symbol of their work was a live birth. The *psychological* aspects of birth were ignored.

In the late twentieth-century all this changed. Interest began to focus upon the quality of the life of the foetus in the womb – with medical engineering at the core – and this produced a whole new dimension to our understanding of human growth and development.

Frederick Leboyer published his *Birth Without Violence* in France in 1974. In it, he poetically portrays this forgotten dimension of what life is like *for the child* within its mother's womb:

> *One day labour starts. The delivery has begun.*
> *Now the child is in the grip of a huge, frenzied, intransigent force.*
> *Curling up is no longer the answer.*
> *Helpless, it huddles up even more tightly. With its head tucked in and its shoulders hunched, it is a compact ball of fright.*
> *The prison has gone berserk, and seems bent on its inmate's destruction. The walls close in still further. The cell narrows hatefully,*
> *and becomes a funnel.*
> *Its heart bursting, the child is thrust into this hell.*
> *Then, suddenly, fear changes to anger.*
> *Enraged, the child hurls itself against the barrier.*
> *At all costs, it must break through. Free itself.*
> *Yet, all this force, this monstrous unremitting pressure that is crushing the baby, pushing it out towards the world, and this blind, blank wall, which is holding it back, confining it – these things are all one:*
> *the mother!* [p.24]

In unforgettable imagery, Leboyer vividly portrays the life and death struggle involved in our birth. While Rank gave us the still, black-and-white 'snapshot' of the trauma of birth, Leboyer produces a moving, technicolour 'video' in all its dynamic, painful horror. There is no doubt in my own mind that this writer, accompanied by his own radical changes in the way in which he cared for the pregnant mothers and their off-spring in his charge in the Paris Faculty of Medicine, has contributed to the most fundamental shift in medical attitudes towards the practice of obstetrics and gynaecology ever seen in the United Kingdom. The whole 'natural childbirth' movement – if not founded by Leboyer – was launched forwards by his searching study. Others, like Michel Odent, [1984] followed in his wake.

Yet even this groundbreaking work of Leboyer is not enough to answer our question: when did I become 'me'? True, we are shaped by the manner of our birth; about that there is no serious doubt. But what of the preceding nine months of gestation? Are intra-uterine experiences *measurable* in terms of what the foetus may be going through?

"Well, naturally", say some medics. "What has our modern technology been about unless for the benefit of the baby and the early diagnosis of possible dangers?" With the invention of the uterine scanners we can see the earliest movements of the foetus – and even carry a photograph home with us of its shape and gender. Yet again, this technology is only concerned with *physical* development and for confirmation that all is (or is not) going according to plan.

But what of the possibility of actual *conscious* awareness *in utero*?

CELLULAR CONSCIOUSNESS AND CONCEPTION

Here we reach the watershed in modern understanding of life within the womb. There are powerful arguments raised against the idea that there is any 'psychological awareness' by the foetus concerning its surroundings. All its movements, so we are told, are merely the result of spasms, automatic responses of the foetus as a purely physical reality. Indeed, we are confidently informed, the foetus actually possesses no means whereby it can process experience in what we would call a mental or psychological way. Thus all is reduced to instinct and reflex. There is still a denial of the very existence of 'uterine memory' – even our vocabulary for such a possibility we have to put in inverted commas and at best is bound to be tentative and partial.

One researcher, David Chamberlain, writes:

> *Memory is expanding along all its borders. Memory does not begin at age two or three but stretches back to birth; newborns have led us to this truth. But memory does not begin at birth; it stretches backward to include prenatal memories as well. In crossing this boundary, it is the unborn who are teaching us. At still farther reaches of memory, even material boundaries have been bridged, as we learn from research into altered states of consciousness.* [*The Expanding Boundaries of Memory*, Pre- and Peri-Natal Psychology Magazine; 4 (3), Spring 1990, p.172.]

There are, of course, equally powerful forces ranged against what they would describe as the naïve and inept assumptions about the nature of 'human awareness' in the womb. However, another researcher who confronts this traditional dismissal is Dr. Graham Farrant, an Australian psychiatrist, who became Director of the Primal Institute in Melbourne. He underwent his own primal therapy during which he had an *"experience of my life as a sperm…but so unaccepted was this in my intellectual mind, let alone my peer medical group…that I did not let on for a few years that what I seemed to be experiencing was existence as a sperm.*" Later on, he experienced a form of existence as the fertilized egg. Comparing the video of his primal experiences with the actual movements of a fertilized ovum, Farrant discovered that they were identical. He found even more, however, about the conjunction of his own 'feelings' at that time of conception and those of his mother.

> *My emotion at the moment (of conception) was a total welcoming, "Come here, Come in!" (Mother's reaction) was a horrible, yecchy, rejecting, "Get out of me, I don't want you" kind of feeling. As I paused to take stock, I felt I had to decide whether I wanted to continue, whether life was worthwhile, if this existence was worth the effort...Although mother's contribution in the energy of the ova is profound, once the new human existence is there in the form of a fertilised egg, it is quite a separate and distinct entity. It is still strongly influenced by the mother's psyche, but has its own set of feelings as well."*
> *[Cellular Consciousness and Conception: An Interview with Dr. Graham Farrant, PPPA Magazine.]*

David Chamberlain adds a further significant note on Farrant's intra-uterine experiences:

> *Many readers will know that Graham Farrant discovered in repeated primals that his mother had attempted to abort him. When he described to her how she had taken a bunch of pills and gotten into a hot tub, she broke into tears and said, "You couldn't know this, I never told anybody." Graham calls these deeply ingrained unconscious memories "cellular" memories.*
> *[op.cit. p.179.]*

In the 1970's, there began a rising tide of literature that addressed this question of cellular consciousness directly. Some of these works were reports of clinical therapy sessions during which – to the total satisfaction of those taking part – both patients and therapists were aware that experiences prior to birth were being relived. It was as if a huge door had swung open giving access to the hitherto unknown and unimagined life within the womb. It is important, at this point, to express how the trained therapists – psychologists and psychiatrists – actually tried different ways in which to interpret the data that was unfolding before their eyes (as Farrant did above). Here were no gullible amateurs imposing their preconceived ideas onto unsuspecting patients. Each of them strove to find alternative ways of interpreting the reports of their patients, until eventually they decided to risk all in publication. These researchers knew the kind of ridicule their reports would receive in the circles of modern medical and psychological studies – and they were not disappointed. They might be – and often were – dismissed as 'unscientific' and relying on anecdotal evidence only. Three pioneer figures stand out as worthy of brief attention.

Stanislav Grof, the Czechoslovakian psychiatrist practising in the USA, was the first to break the silence. His book *The Realms of the Human Unconscious* [1975] related the work he had been doing in the States since 1956, using the hallucinogenic drug LSD25, an abreactive agent.

Two years prior to this, in 1954, an English psychiatrist, **Dr. Frank Lake**, had been using LSD25 as an abreactive agent in clinical therapy. Both Grof and Lake, totally independently, were picking up the same material and it troubled them both. Lake writes, "We both recorded relivings of birth and peri-natal events from the earliest days, though for the first three years I resisted my patients' conviction that this was an actual reliving of their birth." [1981, p.20] It was the third pioneer, however, that actually attracted the greatest attention at the pop-psychology level, **Dr. Arthur Janov**. In 1970, he published his much-acclaimed book, *The Primal Scream.* Although not exclusively depicting intra-uterine experiences, Janov made a breakthrough at a popular level, which challenged head-on the prior medical notion that 'newborn babies remember nothing'. In his later, more technical, works such as *Primal Man: the New Consciousness* [1975] written in conjunction with a neurophysiologist, Michael Holden, Janov dealt with the research into the entire question of the human brain and in particular with the 'levels of consciousness, how they operate, interact and repress.'

The technicality of such issues is not our main concern. These brief introductions will have to suffice as a means of drawing attention to the important aspects of awareness of the foetus in the womb. For if there is some kind of awareness, and I am convinced that there is, then it opens up the whole question of the origins of my own personal identity, and bears upon our important question, "When did I become Me?" Clearly, if I possess (and, under certain conditions, can actually *relive*) primal memories of my existence in the womb then these early traumas bear directly on our question. But how early?

John Rowan writes:

> *Different researchers give different answers to this. Duval and Wicklund (1972) see the major trauma happening at about three years old; Mahler et al (1975) see it happening at about one year old; Klein (Segal, 1979) and the rest of the object relations school put it within the first*

> *six months of life; Grof (1975) and Lake (1966) say that it most often happens at birth, and have a lot of evidence to support their contention; Lake (1966) and Feher (1980) say that it can happen in the womb; Mott (1969) and Laing (1976) say that it can happen at implantation; Sadger (1941) and Peerbolte (1975) say that it can happen as far back as conception; and Netherton and Shiffrin (1979) are willing to go back into past lives in order to find the major trauma which has to be dealt with." [1983, p. 123]*

THE EVIDENCE FROM PRIMAL THERAPY

The growth of Primal Therapy has been one of the most controversial elements in psychotherapeutic intervention over the past three decades. And not without reason, for there are undoubtedly many questions still to be answered. Since much of what I want to say later hangs upon the possibility of 'primal memory' it is important that I consider two sources which confirm this possibility from neurophysiological research.

First, there are the important findings of Dr. Thomas Verny in his book *The Secret Life of the Unborn Child* [1982]. The book is about many things, *"but principally it is about the shaping of the human mind, about how we become who we are."* (p.1) Those readers who are interested in the modern medical research are invited to study this aspect further in Verny's important book.

Secondly, there are the findings of research conducted by a former colleague of mine, the late Dr. Ron Files. In an unpublished paper, *Types of Memory Found in Primal*

Integration and their Use in Therapy (dated 28 June, 1984), he outlines the current research in embryology and zygote formation (the stage of development prior to becoming an embryo), which is largely technical and need not be repeated here. The point to notice, however, is that all current research is revealing deeper and deeper layers of what can only be called in lay terms "foetal memory".

Such memory is stored in the actual chemical consistency of the developing egg, long before the mother is aware that she is pregnant. (The therapeutic value and significance of this is crucial: for it often means that there is a *good* primal memory that acts as an antecedent to later bad memories that may occur in the womb.)

Some patients undergoing Primal Therapy claim to have experienced – that is, actually relived – their own moment of conception (like Graham Farrant mentioned earlier). Others relive their journey as the blastocyst (the developmental phase that succeeds that of the morula, the earliest cluster of cells after conception) as it begins its perilous journey down the Fallopian tube. Some of Frank Lake's patients recall the experience of 'Blastocystic Bliss' (Lake's term) to describe their feelings of freedom and transcendence as a Monistic oneness with the All. Others, however, recall their attempts at implantation with utter terror: "I'm hanging on like grim death," said one patient.

But while there may be other memories, such as an identity with the unfertilised ovum or the sperm itself, it is usually the conjunction of these two elements at conception whereby the fullness of human personality may be said to have its origin. However fanciful this may appear, there is an increasing body of opinion that takes this view as axiomatic. There are huge implications if this is true, not least for the future care of the pregnant mother. Our concern here is to show that I became Me at a time far earlier than most of us would ever have dreamed of. Even (perhaps, especially) the atmosphere of our own conception can have a crucial influence on our later development and concept of selfhood. Common sense – quite apart from the theory of Primal Therapy – would suggest a qualitative difference in outcome from say a child conceived within the horror and violence of a rape, and that of a child conceived in the love and trust of a loving relationship. The possibility – some of us would say, the fact – that the way in which we were conceived can have a significant effect on our later development and concept of selfhood is almost mind-blowing. Yet any theory of personal development that ignores this possibility is, in my opinion, sadly deficient.

For instance, a standard textbook – *Human Development: An Introduction to the psychodynamics of growth, maturity and ageing*, by Eric Rayner [revised in 1986] shows no knowledge of the work of Grof, Lake or Janov and begins his otherwise hopeful chapter on "Being Pregnant" with a sole concern for the mother, (e.g. "Early Pregnancy, the Mother's Experience", p.15). Another writer, Michael Jacobs, in his *The Presenting Past* [1986] – a title which cries out for at least a recognition of the way in which primal pain re-emerges in later life – ignores any significance of intrauterine experiences. Indeed, it is surprising to read as late as 1986, "*Very few people have memories of being a baby...it is very difficult to imagine a state of being unborn...The new-born baby, however, has no frames of reference.*" [Jacobs, op.cit. p.30]

(Since I have worked closely with Michael Jacobs for many years, I know he is not ignorant of the theories of Grof, Lake and Janov, yet it would have been useful to have shown some knowledge of them in his book – even if he dismisses them.)

STEP BY STEP MODEL OF GESTATION

Fay Weldon, throughout her fascinating book *Puffball* [1980] gives a running commentary on what happens inside a woman following sexual intercourse, culminating in the birth of her child. For example:

> *Meanwhile some forty million of Richard's sperm were starting their migration from the vault of Liffey's vagina to the outer part of her fallopian tubes...Richard's sperm, now in Liffey's left fallopian tube, had there encountered a fully fledged ovum, some five hours old and in good shape. By virtue of the enzymes that they carried, en masse, they liquefied the gelatinous material that encased the ovum, enabling one of their number to penetrate the ovum wall, running into head first, leaving its tail outside. And there, Liffey was pregnant. [pp.104-106]*

There follows throughout *Puffball* the story of the developing foetus, and for those of you who would like to pursue the varied and significant stages of uterine development you could read Fay Weldon's account in full with great profit. For our purposes in this chapter, it is important that we recognise the significance of such development to our future identity.

OUR OWN BEGINNINGS

In some such way, during an act of sexual intercourse, the majority of us came into being. (*In vitro* fertilisation may raise other issues but they lie outside the confines of this book.) It is now widely recognised that the 'where, when and how' of our conception is not only all-important but also could possibly determine our future development and identity. The state of our minds affects our bodies in all kinds of ways – emotional feelings, of, say embarrassment, can show themselves physically in blushing, while anxiety can produce restricted breathing. The mental and the physical processes of the human condition are closely interwoven and inextricably linked together, and form what psychologists call 'psychosomatic symptoms'. Nowhere is this link more important than in the complex chemical, emotional and physical conjunctions when sexual intercourse takes place that – a few hours later – issues in a conception. Will Schultz, one of the many writers and therapists involved in the Human Potential Movement, writes of his own attitude before the conception of his child, Ari:

> *Parenting begins before conception. Conception is the point at which life begins. The circumstances surrounding conception undoubtedly have an important influence on the fetus and, ultimately, on the child. Ideally, parents should start planning for the child before conception. [1979, p. 197]*

Schultz goes on to explain how he and his partner prepared for the conception of their child:

> *For my latest child, Ari, conception must have been a unique experience. His mother had fasted on water only for 22 days. I had fasted for 34 days. The first time we made love after the fasts, Ari was conceived. Although my objectivity could be faulted, it seems to me that Ari is a particularly clear and radiant child. I would certainly*

> *recommend something similar to all prospective parents. Fast, or otherwise purify your physical body – exercise, get plenty of sunshine and fresh air, be well rested, be physically fit, and deal with the emotional problems, both individually and interpersonally, between parents. In short, be in first-class condition in every respect just prior to conception. This may be the most important gift you give to your child. [ibid]*

While some of us may find his preparation rather extreme, nevertheless Schultz raises some important issues concerning a neglected part of child-rearing, namely the preparation of the parents. There are, in fact, many people taking this aspect into consideration prior to the conception of their children.

If the act of conception is important, so too is the ongoing development that takes place in the womb over the next nine months. Within the first twelve weeks, extraordinary changes are taking place as the fertilized egg moves from a single cell to a complex one, from an ovum to a morula, from a morula to a blastocyst when the next huge hurdle involves the issue of *implantation.*

If our first 'experience' of encounter is the conjunction of the mother and father's forty-six chromosomes at conception, our first 'journey' is that as the blastocyst down the lining of our mother's fallopian tube. Such processes have now been filmed in amazing detail as shown in Dr. Derek Bromhall's film, *The World of the Unborn Child* and for the first time they are depicted with breathtaking detail how the blastocyst is wafted down the fallopian tube. Dr. R. D. Laing writes, "*Before eventual definitive implantation there may be many adventures. This journey to implantation may form a template for subsequent patterns. As implantation may be mapped onto birth.* [1976. p.45] So, the next major hurdle is implantation, for unless this is negotiated successfully there will be no pregnancy. Of course, in the natural course of things, many such blastocysts make no connection with the lining of the mother's uterus and pass out without the mother knowing she had ever conceived.

But for those blastocysts that do manage a successful implantation there is the primal experience of *attachment*. The whole outcome of the pregnancy depends upon this attachment being negotiated successfully. Later on in the pregnancy, our secondary attachment would be by the development of the umbilical cord to mother's placenta.

One man, reliving such primal memories *in utero*, complained how his life seemed to be 'hanging by a thread'. These feelings were compounded by a total denial on the part of the mother that she was pregnant, a denial she kept up throughout the pregnancy in spite of all the physical signs to the contrary. No matter what we think of such Primal memories, it seems to me to be common sense to be able to distinguish between the experiences of a child in a womb whose mother's welcome is open, warm and generous and one whose mother denies its very existence. Such differing attitudes result in chemical effects in the body itself, and it cannot be denied (except by a prejudiced mind) that they have profound influence on the sense of 'well-being' in the developing child.

Many people living today survived in spite of such harrowing experiences of being denied or rejected at conception. But they have paid a high price for such survival. Some find their way into therapy where they discover, often – if not always – to their utter amazement, that such primal memories are recallable. One will say, "It's as if I'm not here at all!", while another may say, "I've felt rejected by my mother for as long as I can remember". To be fair to pregnant mothers at this point, they are often facing rejection themselves, as in the case of many teenage pregnancies during the Second World War (1939-1945).

Many of such children subsequently born under those circumstances are now in their own later lives, but as part of their Mid-life Transition may have come into therapy to do work on their neurotic defence patterns. Some of them describe themselves as "I must be bad", or, "I feel that I've done something shameful and must be punished for it, but I don't know what it is!" What they do not know at this point is that they are expressing with concise accuracy, not their own feelings, but *those of their mother* but which *they* have carried since their conception. The family rejection of the teenage mother, for example, is 'carried' by the foetus as if it were its own.

Small wonder some of us find the whole notion of 'attachment' so hard to handle in later life. What is hidden from the conscious mind, though totally 'remembered' by the unconscious, is that their primal attachment to the wall of their mother's uterus was tricky, uncertain, or risky. Those of us with such primal experiences will usually find other scenarios of 'attachment' presenting us with identical feelings, e.g. intimacy. In terms of relationships, they may present as standoffishness, withdrawn, holding back or detached altogether. They will have no rational answer to these feelings. One woman said to me concerning her husband, "But I love him so much; why should I detach myself from him?"

A very suggestive model created by the late Dr. Frank Lake has supplied a convincing answer:

THE MATERNAL-FOETAL DISTRESS SYNDROME

This was offered as a model for understanding individual needs, with especial reference to anger, violence, fears, doubts and anxieties, but also as the hermeneutic or interpretative principle for our understanding of the origins of disorders. [The full treatment of Lake's theories lies outside the scope of my present purpose and those who are interested in the details are referred to the work of Lake's biographer, John Peters, 1989].

But in essence, Lake maintains – with thousands of hours of recorded clinical evidence to back up his theories – that the foėtus is vulnerable to all that is happening to the mother, both regarding her outer circumstances and her inward reactions to external events. Lake says:

> *What we...have become firmly convinced about only as we have been able to pay attention to even earlier sources of pain, is the vulnerability of the foetus to all that is going on in the mother, particularly in the first trimester (three months)....the foetus is evidently put into direct contact with all that is being transmitted round the mother's own body as an expression of her own emotional ups and downs. The foetus feels acutely the feelings which are the product of the mother's life situation, for better or worse, and her personal reactions to it. Before she knows that she is pregnant, the foetus knows what sort of person this is, in whom he or she is fortunate or fated to be... Before birth, the foetus may be seriously damaged if the mother is dependent on alcohol, nicotine or other drugs. It is also damaged by the less readily identifiable changes*

> *that transmit to the baby a mother's rejection of a particular pregnancy and of the life growing within her. Any severe maternal distress, whatever its cause, imprints itself on the foetus.* [1981, pp.15/16]

This 'maternal-foetal distress syndrome' opens up possibilities that many of our own patterns of behaviour are the direct result of what was taking place for us *in utero.* Throughout the pregnancy, therefore, we were all subjected to various kinds of psychological influences against which we were, on the whole, defenceless. Unable to prevent the influx of pain and stress, now conveyed through the umbilical cord, the foetus can only employ limited means of warding off the harmful effects conveyed directly to it by mother's emotional state. Those of us who have undergone our own primal therapy, or who have facilitated others in their own journey back to the womb, cannot deny the evidence of our own eyes. As incredible as it may sound, it is both harrowing and awe-inspiring to witness a grown adult re-enacting their experiences within the womb. Of course, adult language is used to describe what in the first instance was *pre-verbal.* And yet the parallel process between the influx of maternal distress and the person's later feelings and elaborate defence system are well nigh undeniable. John Rowan comments:

> *...the real self...was buried and put away as being too weak and too vulnerable for everyday life. We put it away – very often in a moment of panic or terror – because that seemed the only way to survive. [1983, p.63]*

Of course, there are also feelings of bliss and well-being experienced by the developing foetus. Often these are recalled by patients in primal therapy whose intra-uterine development was a reflection of their mother's contentment and nourishment and the support and love she received while she was pregnant. Such experiences, however, are usually unfolded as a precursor to the sudden changes to which not only life, but the mother's life in particular, is susceptible. In my own therapy, I experienced with total self-satisfaction a sense of my own worth and value; my therapist recalls me giggling with joy. However, this did not last. I then experienced the terror of being turned in the womb since the doctors considered (incorrectly, as it turned out) that I was carrying 'the wrong way round'. All my life I had carried with me the unconscious feelings of outrage when they had to turn me back to the original position. I recall shouting out, "I was right all the time!" and was overwhelmed by feelings of total vindication. I had carried those feelings of 'being in the wrong' all my life up to that point. At last, I could get in touch with their origins, and hand them back to my medical mismanagement where they truly belonged. I have rarely had those feelings since my therapy. I, of course, still experience '*doing* wrong' but no longer the crippling, existential feeling of '*being* wrong'.

GETTING THE PAST OUT OF YOUR PRESENT

This personal illustration brings us to the important point of primal *scripts*. 'Scripts' are the sum of our past experiences and they not only exert unconscious pressures upon us; they also influence our own self-perception.

To the extent that we have been influenced – and, in all probability, damaged – by our primal experiences, it is important that we learn how to gain freedom from their often debilitating effects. This process is sometimes called 'getting the past out of your present'. The rest of this book will try to give practical suggestions how this may be done. The following table is offered as a way of connecting with destructive primal scripts so that we may find ways of making vital *dis*connections from their damaging effect upon our lives.

The Primal Script	**Its Damaging Effect**	**Making the Disconnection**
I am unwanted	Feeling that we are a nuisance only tolerated never welcomed	Maybe these were the feelings of mother? If so, give them back
I am in the way	Never feeling comfortable with others; antisocial; 'people better off without me' = excuse for suicide	Perhaps pregnancy an embarrassment? 'In the way' of mother's (or her parents?) career or social prospects? I have the right to BE
If it weren't for me!	Maternal blaming of all subsequent woes on to me: 'I've ruined her life!'	I didn't make the choice to come into being – she and my father did. I refuse to take the blame for their choice
I am feeling ignored and denied	Insatiable desire for constant attention; Acting out to gain attention of others	Maybe my presence was ignored and denied by my parents? These feelings are not mine – I'm carrying them for mother. Let go!

I feel so unsafe and insecure	Acting towards others in a highly dependent manner; no sense of confidence; timid and fearful (phobic)	No warm, accepting maternal feelings; primal fear of not surviving. But we did! The fear is now over
I feel so negative all the time	Critical, judgmental towards others and self; fault-finder, nothing positive in life; pessimistic	Maternal/parental negative feelings towards pregnancy. Carrying these scripts that are not mine. Hand them back!
I am worthless	Chronic sense of inferiority, no sense of personal value or worth; sabotage any worth; sabotages any of my achievements	Maybe scripts put onto mother by family ('shameful, bad, slag, disgraceful'?) They were not talking about me! OK?

LETTING GO OF THE PAST

This is just a small sample of the primal scripts that we can carry from our conception, but they may serve our purpose in showing how they can affect us for most of our lives. Perhaps some of them sound familiar? They play an important role in the way we answer our question, "Who do you think you are?" For, if these primal scripts are left unrecognised and unchallenged, we are destined to go on living out our lives with faulty programming. But how do we let them go?

In one sense, of course, these scripts are part of us – part of our past. There is no way in which they are just going to evaporate. We cannot even go back and erase our past. But that does not mean that we cannot claim power over our past and learn to nullify its deadly effects upon us. The clue to letting go of the past is to *become aware* how far we are having our present lives controlled by these past events. This process of awareness is like putting two and two together, making connections between our primal scripts and our present behaviour pattern. This is how one person made this connection and how she began the process of letting go.

ONE WOMAN'S STORY

Marie Cardinal, in her moving story - *The Words to Say It* [1984] - tells of her harrowing journey through psychoanalysis. It includes a striking confirmation of Frank Lake's 'Maternal-Foetal Distress Syndrome'.

Out of the blue one day, Marie's mother confessed to her futile attempts to induce a spontaneous abortion shortly after Marie had been conceived, in the middle of her parents' divorce. Marie could not have guessed at the horrendous effect such a disclosure would have upon her. Her mother told her:

> *There exist evil women and evil doctors who can do away with a baby in a woman's womb. It's a monstrous sin which the Church punishes with hell-fire...It is possible, however, to lose the baby naturally. A shock can be the provocation, or an illness, medication, even food. Then it's no longer a sin, it's nothing, it's an accident, that's all.*

Marie notes her mother's violence, vulgarity and hatred that lay behind the expression on her face. Her mother continued to describe how she went on long bicycle rides, over rough ground, and even jumping and trotting on horseback. She resorted to playing tennis in the hottest part of the day, and swallowing quinine and aspirin 'by the bottle' to induce an abortion, all without success. Eventually, her mother had to accept the inevitable:

> *At last you were born, for it was you whom I was expecting. Almighty God surely punished me for having tried to tamper with nature: it was an occipitofacial presentation. You were born with your whole face forward, instead of presenting only the base of your skull.*

Marie begins to compare her mother's feelings and attitudes about her pregnancy with those that Marie was feeling towards her own 'unborn self'. With horror, Marie recognises how all the tender evidences of the presence of a foetus were utterly revolting to her mother when she herself was being carried. Marie continues:

> *At the last, powerless, resigned, defeated, disappointed, she let me slip out alive into life, the way you let a slip a turd. And what about that little girl/turd coming slowly, face forward, towards the light she saw down there at the end of the narrow, moist passage, at the end of the tunnel? What was going to happen to her on the outside where already she had been so mistreated? Tell me, Mother, did you know that you were pushing her into madness? Did you question it?*

In all therapeutic literature, this is one of the most poignant and painful descriptions of primal pain. As Marie begins to connect her *own* foetal experience with those of her mother during pregnancy, a different story emerged. The feelings of self-loathing and hatred that had pushed Marie into madness were not hers at all! Only within the safety and security of her psychoanalysis, did Marie make the connection:

> *And yet, it was thanks to her beastliness that, on the couch in the little cul-de-sac, I was more easily able to analyse the malaise of my entire former life, the constant anxiety, the perpetual fear, the self-disgust which finally blossomed into madness. Without my mother's acknowledgement I might never have succeeded in going back to the womb, returning to that hated and pursued foetus, which, without knowing it, I had found when I curled up between the bidet and the tub in the obscurity of the bathroom.* [pp.102-106]

With perceptive and heart-rending precision, Marie pieces together the connections between her mother's experiences and her own later development into madness. Not only did Marie come to understand her mother; she also came to understand *herself* and those primal forces that had shaped her. *Her death wish, previously thought to be her own desire for annihilation, she discovered to be that of her mother towards her pregnancy.* She could now hand her mother's script back to her, written in a time of understandable desperation and anguish, and begin her process of disconnection. This experience proved to be the turning point of Marie's own pursuit of life. She need no longer identify herself with that *'hated and pursued foetus'* – a thing of loathing and disgust (a 'turd') – but establish for herself a new and wholesome identity based on the inner core of her own goodness and value.

Bruno Bettelheim, the well-known child psychologist, writes in the Afterword of Marie Cardinal's book:

> *I have known quite a few children who subconsciously were convinced that they were unwanted and who, correctly, suspected that their mothers had tried to abort them. But in the absence of any statement that this had been so, they could never trust their feelings, if for no other reason that to do so would be too destructive to their security and self-respect. Thus they were caught up in an agonising uncertainty about a most important fact of their lives...*
>
> *In analysis she became aware that she (Marie) had taken into herself her mother's disgust with the foetus that had grown inside of her as a "self-disgust which finally blossomed into madness", a madness in which she became "that hated and pursued foetus". Her way of putting it is the best and the most drastic description known to me of this type of madness – the consequences of the internalisation of a mother's death wishes by a child whom she had tried to rid herself of. It is the child's identification with both the foetus the mother felt was disgusting and with the mother's destructive wish to get rid of the foetus which explains the details of the daughter's illness.* [*op. cit.* p.125]

It was only by uncovering the significance of her pregnant mother's wishes that Marie was enabled to leave them behind, rejecting the sense of worthlessness that they had engendered in her, and to begin the process of a discovery of a new sense of worth and self-esteem.

The importance of Marie's story for our present purpose is

that we too may need to pay attention to those lurking feelings within us that may have issued in a sense of worthlessness or negativity. It is just possible that they are based, not on fantasy and imagining, but on *actual history*. In either case, we are now free to dissociate ourselves from their toxic effects upon our lives and to recognise that *they never did belong to us*. They were dumped on us by others; they bear their fingerprints, not ours!

We need to go on, however, to discover what happened to us after our birth, and who were the important family 'script-writers' into whose hands we were placed for better or for worse.

CHAPTER TWO
Theme: Distortion

WHO TOLD ME I WAS ME?

"If a family is a factory for turning out children then it is lacking in the most elementary safety precautions. There are no guard rails round that dangerous engine the father. There are no safeguards against being scalded by the burning affection of the mother. No mask is proof against the suffocating atmosphere. One should not be surprised that so many lose their balance and are mangled in the machinery of love."
[Alan Bennett: 1994, p.338]

In the previous chapter we discussed the important question, 'How did I become Me?' This concerned chiefly our earliest embryonic development and all the influences to which we were subject within the womb.

Of course, 'becoming me' is not an *event*, like a birth; as we shall see, it is a *process* of experiences during which we attain a self-identity. So far in this process we have identified some important 'building blocks' which, by the time we come to be born, are already in place as far as our own self-perception is concerned. I find R. D. Laing's case for our earliest intrauterine experiences being "a template for subsequent patterns" of behaviour totally compelling. However, there are further distorting influences yet to be negotiated as we progress throughout childhood.

In this chapter we move on to ask another important question, 'Who told me I was me?' Even if our earliest, embryonic experiences were, on the whole 'good enough' (to use Donald Winnicott's well-known phrase) we still have to navigate this subsequent phase of our development in the early years of childhood. If the earliest phase went badly, however, then we are already programmed, set-up, and more vulnerable to the onslaughts to come. The arena of this drama is our family unit.

THE LION, THE WITCH AND THE WARDROBE

It seems to me that we can usefully adapt the title of C. S. Lewis's well-known Narnia story as a metaphor for what happens to us in our early childhood. These factors may be individual people ('single-parent' families) or composite realities within our wider nuclear family unit.

The Lion, I suggest, may represent the power brokers, especially the King of the Jungle, the one with the most power in our family, usually father.

The Witch may represent those who were thought of as good and on our side but who proved, like the so-called Queen of Narnia, to be none other that the malevolent White Witch.

The Wardrobe may be used as the container symbol for what our family handed down to us in terms of our self-identity and our role within our family. What we were expected to 'wear' as the price of remaining safe within its domain. Were we given 'rags' to wear, like Cinderella, or were we well dressed like her ugly sisters? What were the messages printed on our infant T-shirts by our family ("Here Comes Trouble") and who landed us with those messages? These are some of the questions that will occupy our attention here.

***The Lion*:**

Somewhere along our developmental path we have encountered a Lion in our family. Perhaps, as happens on occasions, a whole pride of lions? To be the youngest of, say, a family of six, puts us in the lowest place of the family pecking order. To the sixth sibling, the whole family would appear to be a formidable group into which we had to make our way as best we could. By the time we arrived, the family would have achieved an identity of its own, and we were already within the sphere of a tradition governed by nation, culture, language, race, creed and behaviour patterns. The family mould has already been set fast by the time we arrive and the unspoken expectation is that we must conform to its set of values and beliefs.

This is true, to a certain extent, even if we are the only child. In that case, we are the guinea pig, the proto-type child on whom our father and mother are going to experiment at being parents. Apart from the nuclear family, there is the extended family of which we are part. Perhaps it is Grandfather or Grandmother who wears the Lion's mane? Some families throw up a Patriarchal or Matriarchal figure to whose will the family must submit. Somewhere or other, then, power resides outside us; and when the Lion roars we have little choice but to listen and obey and cower.

This external power is, however, perceived by the newborn child in stark contrast to its own sense of weakness, helplessness and vulnerability. When used appropriately, such power can be a haven of rest, and encourage us to find in the family a sense of safety and security. There are strong resources all around us that are available to us when we need them. Without the nurturing family, we will not survive infancy, so there is much to play for by availing ourselves of what is has to offer.

In the nurturing family, the baby is given all that is needed for its physical, psychological and spiritual well-being. Its basic needs are attended to and given priority by the nurturing parents. Warmth, touch, food, sight, and affection are among its basic needs, and the baby soon becomes aware of what kind of family it has around it. All these represent the building-blocks of its own sense of security, and how far it can trust its environment to meet its basic human needs. The baby at this point of its existence (say, 0-6 months) is in a totally dependent state; its very life depends upon other people taking an interest in supplying its basic life-support system. It seems to me that we never forget this early stage of our development, for it is easy to regress back to such feelings later on in life. The reason is simple: at this stage of our life our chief aim is to survive, and the stakes are nothing less than *life or death.*

That issue lies mainly in the hands of the Lion. Who was it that had the power of life and death over me when I was newly born? For many of us in mid-life or beyond, this would almost undoubtedly have been 'mother'. People now between the ages of 60-70 would have been born during World War II or soon after [1939-1945]. Fathers were in short supply. They were serving in the armed forces and many of them were absent for years; sadly, many failed to return. Those years were times of severe stress, danger from enemy bombing and shortages of supplies. Rationing reduced every commodity to a 'coupon value'. Mothers often had to go out to work to make ends meet, leaving babies to fare as best they could with friendly (or, not-so-friendly) neighbours or grandparents. It was a time of national upheaval and one that would later mark the end of a way of life that many had begun to take for granted. This especially affected the 'three-decker' families: children, parents and grandparents either living together or close by.

Post-war developers came by and turned neighbourhood streets on their end, resulting in the 'high-rise' blocks of flats that destroyed family life and good neighbourliness. Community gave way to isolation, and - on the principle of the 'weakest to the wall' - babies were the least able to protect themselves from its worst excesses. Many were robbed of vital contact with the wider family and, to the extent that mother was further isolated particularly in single-parent situations, her child was often a source of anxiety as she struggled to meet its needs from her own depleted resources. Not all mothers, of course, were placed in such conditions. Some had their own families around them to provide support and encouragement and to do their turn of baby-sitting to enable mother to have a well-earned break.

There are well-worn scripts reinforcing the leonine power. Perhaps the oldest and best known is the 'Honour thy father and mother' in the Ten Commandments. It did not appear to matter whether or not father and mother were 'honourable' in their attitudes and behaviour towards us; they still expected us to do as they said and knuckle under to their regime.

Under a provocative title, "Honour thy father and mother: No way" [Observer, 15.9.1991], writer and psychologist Alice Miller was interviewed by Alix Kirsta. Alice Miller's books have been a huge influence in raising the social consciousness concerning the abuse of young children. Kirsta writes, "*...she (Miller) is convinced that the origins of all human destructiveness* *and violence – from street crime to war – can be traced to the injured child's incapacity to express early terror, humiliation, powerlessness and especially fury and outrage against its parents."* Here is the worst aspect of the power of the family lions.

During her own therapy in a period of 'free associative' painting, Alice Miller *"was engulfed by flood upon flood of violent, painful, hitherto damned-up emotions forcing her to remember what she calls the 'terrorism' of her mother. Analysis had failed to reveal any of this...but her canvasses revealed only part of the truth. In the mid-Eighties she encountered a unique new form of primal therapy, devised by a Swiss therapist, J. Konrad Stettbacher, which finally provided what she had been attempting unsuccessfully to find for so many years – complete recall and resolution of all her early trauma."* It is not hard to see, therefore, why Miller rejects the hitherto sacrosanct commandment to 'Honour thy father and thy mother'. It is under this cloak, Miller says, that *"centuries...permitted child-rearing to remain a power game in which any abuse is permitted, while the child's criticism of its parent is forbidden."*

Alice Miller, through her study, practice and the reliving of her past abuse at the hands of her mother, presents a powerful case against the traditional respect demanded by parents. Where parental 'might-is-right' approaches to childcare are applied, untold damage can be done to the vulnerable baby. This does not just involve physical abuse at the hands of the family lions, but psychological and sexual abuse as well. Much of this has only now recently emerged within a climate that is more permissive - and offering for the first time *credibility* - to such stories that in the past have been dismissed as 'fanciful' or, in Freud's term, 'wish-fulfilment'. This raises enormous issues concerning childcare, and there are many welcome signs today – both in the home and school – that some of them are beginning to be addressed. Corporal punishment has largely been both questioned and abandoned as a means of correcting children.

The *psychological* impact of the family lions, however, is much harder to determine. This concerns not so much the family actions but the family *attitudes* towards the child and its own sense of value. Think for a moment about some of the scripts in your own family. What was the basis of its belief system about itself and the world? And with what messages did you emerge from childhood concerning your Self? As you discover these you will be in direct touch with the formative elements in your own personal background. We shall see later on how they continue operating in your life today.

***The Witch*:**

Happy indeed are those who look back on their past only to find it filled with fairy godmothers that took care of their every need. 'Good-enough mothering' is a fundamental right of every child, but unfortunately experience teaches us that many of us have been deprived of this right.

The reasons are legion. Truth to tell, this was not always mother's fault. She herself may have had to cope with a large family, single-handed, perhaps in financial hardship due to her husband's gambling or drinking – or both. In the so-called 'dysfunctional' family, many of the fundamental needs of the children are simply neglected. They have to get by as best as they can. Survival becomes the name of the game.

However, there is a third kind of family – akin to the many fairy-stories we remember from childhood – where the Queen is really a witch in disguise. Things in these families are not always what they seem to be! As Snow White discovered, the rosy apple is found to have deadly poison within it. (Remember

Marie Cardinal's mother [p.27] giving her daughter 'the lovely poisoned brew', a phrase straight out of Snow White?) Or, like the story of Sleeping Beauty, the attractive distaff has a sharp point that will put her to sleep for a hundred years.

The family 'witch', therefore, may have had a benign appearance. What she did to us may have been under the disguise of, "I'm only doing this for your own good..." What ugly events have been explained away under such an apparently benign disguise? No wonder small children get confused. Confused and bewitched. (For those of you with stomachs strong enough to endure it, try reading the story of *Sybil* by Flora Rheta Schreiber, 1973.)

Some witches, of course, are simply sick, like Sybil's mother. Had their toxic influence been discovered earlier they would never have had children entrusted to their care. Fathers, too, can turn a blind eye. But, alas, the family is a very private place where all kinds of evil can pass as normality. A particularly nasty, though by no means unique, illustration was reported in the *Observer* (24.11.91) by 'Ross Connelly'.

Recently...I had a painful flash of revelation. My mother had largely contributed to my early abuse by my father. I didn't want to believe it, but it all made some kind of horrible sense. As a young married woman, I had asked my mother, a staunch Catholic who was against contraception, how it was that at 36 after eight children, she had suddenly stopped producing them. She said, "I just decided I had had enough. I didn't let your father near me after Jim was born".

As a woman of 50 herself, 'Ross Connelly' struggled to come to terms with her father's abuse. She was only four when it began, the only female child of the family. She recalls her mother coaxing her to join her father for his nap after his lunchtime visit to the pub. In spite of curling up under the table in a tight ball, mother said, 'Just go up with him until he drops off; he'll leave some sweeties under the pillow; don't be selfish – it's not for long', and so on.

> *As the only female child in a household of eight males, my responsibility for their happiness had lain like a heavy burden. I had known I was the one who could sweeten my father's mood; the one who could save my brothers from his regular beatings and my mother from his displeasure. So small and yet so powerful... What I had never previously seriously considered was the possibility that my mother had colluded in my abuse...maybe it was a contrived ignorance; maybe all the time he had me she was freed of the necessity to let my father near her.*

The long-term effects of this tragic story included her mother turning away from her. She felt abandoned. So much so, that Ross felt she must be entirely unlovable. Much of Ross's life had been spent trying to find the 'good mother' until eventually she found it in therapy, *"the unconditional, loving acceptance I had always sought; the support I had always needed; the understanding I had craved."*

While such stories are not plentiful – do most of the victims choose to remain in silence in order to cover their shame and misplaced guilt? – there are enough of them around to see one particularly nasty evidence of The Witch at work. Having counselled many such victims, I know of the terror and repulsion with which such women as Ross dare to go into these black areas of their experience. "Honour thy father and thy mother" can produce a paralysing conflict within them.

One woman, in her seventies, told of repeated abuse by her father, both of herself and her sisters, over a period of almost eighteen years. What stood in the way of her allowing her feelings towards her father to emerge was this biblical injunction her father had taught her and the family. (He was a local Church elder.) On one occasion I reached for the bible and quoted another text to my client, "Does not Saint Paul in Romans 13:7 say, 'Honour to whom honour is due'? Are you really telling me your father's behaviour towards you and your sisters was honourable?" This was a possibility that she had never before considered, and it helped her to uncover some of the feelings of rage and pain that had lurked beneath the surface of her life for over fifty years.

Here is an example of the father bewitching his children through a manifestly grotesque use of the scriptures. "It can't be wrong if Daddy is doing it, can it?" the child may ask. Their infant trust in parents does not give way easily, and the reason is not hard to find: they need to trust their safety and security to someone and, in spite of the evidence to the contrary, they will go on trusting even when the parents' behaviour is abominable. The principle seems to be this: *to a child, a bad parent is better than no parent at all.* Yet again, we see the principle of survival governing the actions and belief-system of the infant.

The Witch is a universal symbol, one of the cosmic archetypes of evil, as maintained by Carl Gustav Jung. It is not necessarily a *feminine* preserve although most of the witches in ancient tribal literature are female. Women do not have an exclusive responsibility for evil, even though this is how they have been misrepresented in some patriarchal societies. The process of bewitching always involved a mixture of attraction, charm, deceit and an evil outcome. The blandishments (OED = flattery, coaxing, cajolery) of those in our families can now, in adult life, be exposed for what they were. We may wonder how we were ever duped by them. Nevertheless we probably were 'bewitched'. Children are usually trusting of adults to want the best for them and it is this basic trust – a vital component for their future development – that constantly gets damaged or destroyed. Small wonder there are so many damaged adults around.

They are victims of the Lion and the Witch.

But there is even further evidence of this damage. For this, we must look inside our personal and family wardrobe. For if –

the Lion represents *an abuse of power*, and
the Witch represents *an abuse of trust*, then
the Wardrobe represents *an abuse of our individuality*

– this may account for the legacy of pain, humiliation and low self-esteem that we have, like ill-fitting clothing, probably 'worn' for most of our lives.

The Wardrobe

One way of understanding the meaning and significance of the wardrobe is to examine the clothes that we find inside. We shall probably find that, like most children's wardrobes, everything inside has been provided by other people. The sinister implication for us is that, whereas our physical body grows and old clothes have to be discarded, psychologically we may be stunted and find ourselves wearing those clothes – and, significantly, the identity that they convey – forever. As Lucy discovered:

> *...there was a second row of coats hanging up behind the first one. It was almost quite dark in there and she kept her arms stretched out in front of her so as not to bump*

> *her face into the back of the wardrobe...But she could not feel it. "This must be a simply enormous wardrobe!" thought Lucy, going still further in and pushing the soft folds of the coats aside to make room for her...A moment later she found that she was standing in a the middle of a wood at night-time with snow under her feet and snowflakes falling through the air.* [1950, p.12]

The wardrobe is C. S. Lewis's literary symbol for access to another world, significantly the land of Narnia ruled over by the Queen who was really The White Witch. The snow depicts a permanent winter: *"Always winter in Narnia – always winter, but it never gets to Christmas!"* Perhaps by looking inside your own family 'wardrobe' you, like Lucy, will be able to discover clues to your childhood world? More importantly, what did those significant others in your family – the lions and the witches – decide what you were going to have to wear? We often use the phrase, "I'm not wearing that!" in a figurative way when others are trying to ascribe to us attitudes or beliefs that are not our own.

Before I was born, my mother desperately wished for a baby girl, having already given birth to my older brother, Peter. She even had my name ready: Pamela. My gender must have come as a disappointment to her hopes, but she still had a card or two to play. She let my hair grow into long curls, and even at the age of two she dressed me in girls' clothes. In the early nineteen-thirties, long baby clothes were not very unusual, but eventually my father began to smell a rat! He confronted my mother about her behaviour, my hair was cut and I was promptly put into boys' clothing. My Dad knew nothing about Freud, but he could see how inappropriate my mother's behaviour was and warned her that I could "grow up to be a cissy" unless she changed her attitude. (Thanks, Dad!)

The array of clothing found in our family wardrobe is quite often bewildering. It may contain, like mine, clothing belonging to the wrong gender. But let us look at some of the other costumes they may contain:

The Clown

There is no mistaking the clown's outfit – large, baggy trousers, garish make-up and the red nose. "He's such a scream!", says father. "She's always fooling around!", says mother. Some of us may have had the role of clown thrust upon us; maybe on occasions it was a role we actually chose for ourselves in order to 'fit in'. Historically, the clown has an interesting story. The medieval festival, known as The Feast of Fools, was celebrated about the first of January, and was a popular device whereby *"even ordinarily pious priests and serious townsfolk donned bawdy masks, sang outrageous ditties, and generally kept the whole world awake with revelry and satire. Minor clerks painted their faces, strutted about in the robes of their superiors, and mocked the stately rituals of church and court. Sometimes a Lord of Misrule, a Mock King, or a Boy bishop was elected to preside over the events."* [Harvey Cox, 1969, p.3] The whole festival died out during the dour attitudes adopted during the Protestant Reformation in the sixteenth century yet lives on in some contemporary New Year's Eve parties and pranks.

For some, however, there was a whole clown's outfit placed in our wardrobe by those who designated us the family fool. Many of us have been wearing it ever since. The evidence comes out in a variety of ways.

First, there is the grease paint, the make-up that clowns wear. Make-up covers up our real face and presents a distorted image, not an accurate reality. Our permanent smile or grin conveys a happy-go-lucky attitude to life – "Problems? What problems?" Clowns are nice to have around, they project a very positive attitude to life – the life and soul of parties and they bring sunshine into people's lives. People like clowns.

With the make-up and the false face, go the clothes clowns wear. They are bright, garish, and unconventional. There is no missing a clown in a crowd! They make people laugh, and even when they do fall down, they usually bounce back with a smile. Clowns are blessed with a carefree attitude and usually have a crowd around them. In families, the clown acts the part of the person who never quite grows up and never learns to take life seriously. They are usually children at heart themselves, which is why children love them.

There is, of course, another side to the clown's existence. Who is the real person underneath the mask and the grease paint and the gaudy clothes? Ruggero Leoncavallo (1858-1919) was a Neapolitan opera composer whose chief claim to fame rests on his opera *Pagliacci* ("Clowns"). The story line concerns a troupe of travelling players of whom Canio is the leader. He warns that if ever he should find his attractive wife (Nedda) had been unfaithful to him, she would pay dearly for it. However, Nedda and her lover, Silvio (the Baritone, naturally) plan to run away together. Canio gives vent to his grief and

> *"in the play put on for the villagers [in which he – Canio - takes the part of Pagliacco, Nedda that of Columbine, and Beppe that of Harlequin] he finds the situation so like reality that he stabs first Nedda, and then Silvio, who rushes to her aid."* [New Oxford Companion to Music, Vol. 2, OUP, 1984, p.1383]

No one who has ever heard great tenors like Enrico Caruso or

Placido Domingo singing the part of Canio ("Vesti la Giuba") can fail to be moved by the sheer pathos of this story: A clown whose heart is breaking inside while he has to go on with the show. Leoncavallos's story, however, is by no means confined to opera. A similar story is found in countless real life situations where the outward and inward realities are at odds. Perhaps we have known such moments in our own families? We dare not let the mask slip and 'spoil the show'. In order to cope with such conflict we often resort to the familiar defence of 'denial'; easier to deny that we hurt than let our mask slip and embarrass others at the sight of our pain. Perhaps our very acceptance within our family depended upon our 'keeping up appearances'? We are conditioned by families to 'always look on the bright side of life'. Indeed such deception is seen as a virtue!

Laugh, though your heart is breaking;
Smile, though your heart is aching...

The British (in particular) have turned such a vice into a national virtue. Showing our true feelings is deemed to be 'letting the side down' and – worse still – a definite sign that we are 'Not Coping'. So, today we will still go to our wardrobe and put on our clown's outfit in order to please other people. And, as Sheldon Kopp perceptively points out, "sometimes I take off a mask worn too long only to discover that I dare not throw it away because part of my face is still in it!" [1987, p.211]

The Dunce

This is a catch-all phrase representing the role of the family idiot, the stupid one, the 'dimmy', the 'slow' one, the 'thicko'. The synonyms are endless. Perhaps there was a T-Shirt that was handed down to us by our family: on it were the words, "I am the Family Idiot".

Some of us have forgotten that we are still wearing this T-Shirt. Heaven knows, we should have grown out of it by now. But no. These wardrobes (remember?) are magical and, unless we consciously remove it, the T-Shirt simply grows as we grow. The evidence of the Dunce identity is conveyed in a variety of ways to the people who really listen.

The clue is the way in which people wearing this particular part of their wardrobe *speak about themselves*. Here is a selection that I have heard:

> I know I'm silly, but…
> I'm so stupid…
> I'm the family thicko…
> You'll think I'm daft, but…
> I expect I've got this all wrong, but…
> I'm so sorry, I'm not very clever…
> My mum used to say I'm as daft as a brush…
> Dad used to call me barmy…
> I'm the brainless wonder…

The way in which we tend to diminish ourselves in front of other people is usually a well-learned process by the time we reach our teenage years. By then, we are describing ourselves in terms such as these and eventually we lose all consciousness that we are doing so. It merely becomes a habit. Any praise or admiration is usually sidestepped and (subconsciously) denied. On the other hand, we will step in to accept blame even in situations where it is manifestly not our fault. All our natural gifts and talents are either under-used or made light of. (In my own family, my natural talents were put down to being 'a Gough'!)

Such is our conditioning that we are taught to play down any accomplishments as either a fluke or due to the over-generosity of other people. This is a distortion of a person's natural goodness and it can happen in a number of ways.

A member of our family, for example, may have been selected as the 'clever one'. There must be no competition to interfere with such a selection, however unconscious the process may be. A promising piano player may be made to transfer to the violin so as not to compete with another sibling's piano prowess. Their wardrobe represents the roles chosen for them in childhood and since most of us do not know we are still 'wearing' these roles, we do nothing to discard them. The wardrobe becomes a sinister symbol for the family *status quo*. When all fails, we are warned that we are in danger of falling into that sin of all sins: having 'a Big Head'. That is usually enough to send us back into our 'dunce' role. Some educators have reinforced this role in former times when the children were made to stand in a corner with a dunce's hat on.

The Little Professor

Sometimes this negative self-image is not always tolerable, even at a subconscious level. Our natural human defence systems can then come into operation and we begin to conceal this sense of distortion by even more distortion! The person taught that he was stupid may adopt a 'wise role' and act out in a pretentious way knowledge that he does not actually possess. He or she becomes the 'Barrack-Room Lawyer' who purports to know everything about everything. The pub quiz is their natural habitat. The 'stupid' image becomes so intolerable that it gets hidden behind a 'wise' one! What they do not know is that both images are distortions of their true Self. The result emerges in a further character that we can call The Little Professor.

This character can be identified by noticing grown-up clothing in this child's wardrobe. He (though it may be she) looks rather pathetic, with long baggy trousers, sleeves that drop beneath his fingers and a top hat only kept on his head by his ears! In dressing-up games he could look laughable, yet at least he knows that he's wearing clothing inappropriate to his size. He eventually takes them off. But the child, defending against his parents' 'stupid' scripts, may not acknowledge that he is now wearing adult clothing and making pretensions to adult knowledge that is far in advance of his years. He may attract the label of 'precocious', sometimes exhibiting a degree of sophistication way beyond his capacity to sustain. Chances are this is the only way in which the child can survive. He will prove to his parents that he is not stupid, and his survival skills are now concentrated upon the attainment of *knowledge* and his supremacy over sibling rivals or peer group. The 'stupid' image, that his parents may have projected upon him at first, will now be projected by this child on to his brothers and sisters – a sinister game of 'pass the parcel'. He will pretend to some exasperation when his siblings show any sign of ignorance. "When will you ever learn?" he may sigh with obvious irritation. They never admit to mistakes (perish the thought!) and become hardened against any insights into their true ability. Little Professors sometimes grow up to become actual professors, and make a good job of it. Humanity has a surprising way of creating good out of evil.

Little Professors are usually intolerable of other people's faults, and blind to their own. They become deaf to reason and unable to hear both sides of an argument. Theirs is the only view worth maintaining. They become bigots. "No good talking to him; he never listens!"

Another aspect of this role is that Little Professors are able to live in 'their heads' and not in 'their hearts'. In other words, they suppress their true feelings. They become cerebral, not visceral, in their approach to life. When asked what they are feeling, they reply, "I think..." They are in the habit of *feeling* with their heads, not their hearts. In therapy, this can be confronted, but only in order to raise the awareness of the client's unconscious pattern of behaviour. In families, we try to ignore them.

Sweet Little Girl

Here is the genesis of the stereotyped little girl. She is made up of 'sugar and spice and all things nice.' So far, so good. The parental influences have a mental image of how their daughter *should* look and behave. She is, accordingly, groomed to fit in with the image projected on to her by her parents. 'Nice little girls don't do that!' 'Good little girls don't wear things like that!' 'Nice little girls don't speak to Mummy like that!' Such programming goes far beyond lessons on behaviour, apparel or speech. These injunctions have little to do with politeness; they are part of a destructive pattern known as 'systematic conditioning'.

What becomes of all those things within this little girl that are deemed to be 'not nice' - her natural capacities to romp and get dirty and shout and lose her temper and have a tantrum or climb a tree? All these must be suppressed in order to maintain the stereotypical image her parents have chosen. There is nothing here about allowing the child to become who she is; there is everything here about a blatant programme of moulding and indeed 'brainwashing'. One such person confronted me in my counselling room.

She walked in as if she'd just stepped off the front page of Vogue magazine. She was vivacious, had an immaculate hairdo, and I felt assaulted by her disarming smile. As is my wont with new clients, I jotted down in my notes what I was most immediately aware of: "Watch that smile!" As her story unfolded, it was obvious that much pain and hurt lay below the surface of this perfect image. Not once did the smile quiver; it was quite unreal. At the end of her story, tears were streaming down her face, and still the smile did not falter. I gently drew her attention to the incongruent picture before me: 'Your smile and your tears don't seem to match, do they?', I offered. Back came the conditioned reply: "People don't like girls who don't smile". "Who taught you that?" I asked. "Oh", she said, "My mother". I risked another response: "You know, I'd prefer an honest frown to that dishonest smile!" The mask suddenly crumbled, and she allowed her mouth to assume a more appropriate downward turn as she sobbed out the rest of her painful story.

The unspoken message that had been instilled into her since childhood was, "You are unacceptable if you don't smile!" In my room, within a therapeutic 'unconditional positive regard', for the first time in her life she met an adult who was prepared to challenge that 'nice little girl' script and invite an honest expression of her feelings. She was able to accept my offer of acceptability in the open expression of her pain, rather than continue the confidence trick perpetrated on her by her mother. What lay behind her continuation of this childhood conditioning, of course, was the terror of finding herself rejected. It is not easy to let go of such conditioning; after all, they may say, 'it's worked for me so far'. Yet, again and again, we find that what once may have been a means of our survival in childhood becomes a millstone around our necks in adulthood. Her mask that may have helped her to survive was now destroying her.

There are healthy signs that such stereotypical attitudes towards gender in general, and girls in particular, are changing, however. The Women's Movement begun in the last quarter of the twentieth century has challenged most of them head-on, and encouragingly many of their insights are now being taken for granted.

Brave Little Boy

The equivalent male stereotype for little boys is that of the strong soldier – the warrior. He is (psychologically) dressed in battle fatigues, desert boots and has an Armalite or an AK-47 rifle in his hands. Uniforms, guns, helmets, and weaponry abound in the little boy's wardrobe. Sam Keen offers his usual mixture of realism and perception into this state of affairs in which many boys are raised:

> *Because men have historically been the major agents of violence, it is tempting to place the blame on our biology and to conclude that the problem lies in nature's faulty design rather than in our wilfulness. But all deterministic explanations ignore the obvious: men are systematically conditioned to endure pain, to kill, and die in the service of the tribe, nation, or state. The male psyche is, first and foremost, the warrior psyche. Nothing shapes, informs, and molds us so much as society's demand that we become specialists in the use of power and violence, or as we euphemistically say, "defence".*
>
> *Historically, the major difference between men and women is that men have always been expected to be able to resort to violence when necessary. The capacity and willingness for violence has been central to our self-definition. The male psyche has not been built upon the*

> *rational, 'I think; therefore I am' but upon the irrational 'I conquer, therefore I am'.* [1991, p.36f]

Sam Keen's assessment goes to the heart of the problem. There is a universal, cultural and tribal expectation about the way in which little boys should be brought up. It is expecting the impossible that individual families should escape the infection of such widespread social expectations. In brief: boys are to be defined as *not being girls.*

The seriousness of this state of affairs is to be seen in the fact that, not only do many of us bring up our sons in a qualitatively different manner from our daughters, but that we are no longer conscious of doing so. It has become part of the accepted way of doing things. Little girls who fall down and graze their knees are to be comforted; little boys who do the same may be greeted with, "Don't be a cry-baby; big soldiers don't cry!" – or more briefly, "You woos!" Expressions of feelings become, thereby, the sole preserve of the feminine species. After all, most men are brought up by women! I had often pondered on this state of affairs, how was it that if we are brought up by caring mothers, many men turn out to be so unfeeling. One day, the answer came to me during a counselling session.

I had been seeing "Sam" for some time. He was thoroughly depressed and on the edge of a complete nervous breakdown. He longed for his wife to take his condition seriously and to make some move towards him in a caring way. Instead, she was keeping her distance. He illustrated this by saying that, one day on his return home, he burst into tears and asked her to hold him. "Not now, Sam", she said, "I'm cooking dinner!" I reminded her of this encounter when we had the first joint session together. Her reply has stayed with me ever since. "I can't be doing with weak men!" she said coldly.

Here – or so it seemed to me at the time – was the authentic mother's voice heard in families for millennia. In 'not doing with weak men', could it be that mothers are themselves guilty of raising their sons in the image of Rambo? Could some of the strident feminine voices raised against the violence and lack of emotion in men belong to those that produced these warriors in the first place? Have women (and men!) become hoist on their own petard?

Of course, this could be seen as a 'no-win' situation. For how else could their strong little boys survive amongst other strong little boys? Maybe mothers are doing the only thing they can for their sons by raising them in the warrior mode? The implications of such issues are far beyond my present purpose but I raise them in order to make a plea for a thoroughgoing questioning of current stereotypes of both little boys and little girls. Indeed, there are many hopeful signs that this is happening. For example, the so-called 'draft-dodgers' in America during the Vietnam War were largely reviled in that country as 'unpatriotic' and even 'cissies'. Indeed, they took an enormous risk in *not* following the 'warrior expectations' of their culture. At least some of them were prepared to throw their battle fatigues out of their inherited wardrobes.

I knew change was in the air when one of my teenage granddaughters arrived wearing a T-Shirt with the Logo: *I love my attitude problem!*

HOW TO CHANGE FROM WEAKNESS TO STRENGTH

With such an array of power stacked against us as very young children, how could we not have been drastically affected by its influence? Our weakness and vulnerability were abused by the power of the lions, our basic trust was abused by the wiles of the family witch, and the keepers of our personal wardrobe abused our individuality. Having passed through such a wounding and distorting process, it is any wonder that there could be anything left of our true selves.

This is not to say that every parent is evil in his or her intent towards his or her infants. Most of them are decent, caring people who only wish the best for them. And herein lies the danger: if decent, caring parents can perpetrate such distortions upon their children, what hope is there for those children whose parents simply don't care enough? Those who are raised in deprived and dysfunctional families have even less of a chance of escaping the family mould. All current sociological studies show that, unchecked and undiscovered, they grow up to produce even more families after their own pitiful pattern. In the end, it is hard to distinguish the victims from the villains.

In her helpful book *Toxic Parents*, Dr. Susan Forward says:

> *A toxic parent's beliefs about children...are almost always self-centred and self-serving. They believe things like, 'children should respect their parents no matter what'; 'there are only two ways to do things, my way and the wrong way'; or, 'children should be seen and not heard'. These types of belief form the soil from which toxic parental behaviour grows. Toxic parents resist any external reality that challenges their beliefs. Rather than change, they develop a distorted view of reality to support the beliefs they already have. Unfortunately, children lack the sophistication to discriminate between true reality and distorted reality. As children of toxic parents grow*

up, they carry their parents' distorted beliefs unchallenged into their own adult lives. [1989, p.167]

ILLUSTRATIONS FROM LITERATURE

Much of the literature quoted so far has encapsulated many home truths that have been examined in this chapter. C. S. Lewis is a case in point, particularly in his *Tales of Narnia.* They contain the fairly consistent mythical themes of 'Captivity', 'Power' (either witch or lion), 'Victim' (usually female) and 'Rescuer' (usually male). There is also a Journey to take or a 'Trial' of some kind before making the journey home to we are.

We could benefit from reading some of these stories in order to see, from the point of view of this present book, how some of the problems of life were eventually resolved. We may take *The Wizard of Oz* as an example.

It is not hard to find the power-people in this magical book by Lyman Frank Baum (first published in 1900). There is a Wizard of Oz (a rather vague figure until Dorothy reaches the Emerald City) and four witches, two of them good and two of them bad. On arrival in the land of the Munchkins, Dorothy meets the Good Witch of the North who tells her of the Great Wizard of Oz, more powerful than all the witches and wizards. After all the events on her journey, immortalized in the film featuring Judy Garland, Dorothy eventually reaches the great Palace of Oz. The throne room was empty and only a solemn voice announces, "I am Oz, the Great and Terrible..." Dorothy, the Tin Man, the Lion and the Scarecrow (plus Toto the dog) are in the presence of ultimate power, and all the people stand in awe of him.

And then, to the amazement of everybody, Toto runs off in

alarm and tips over a screen standing in the corner of the throne room. As it falls, who should be revealed but a little old man, with a bald head and wrinkled face. He declares himself to be "Oz, the Great and Terrible.." - or at least he is supposed to be! The Scarecrow blurts out that he is a humbug and the Wizard admits that he is 'just a common man,' a ventriloquist who uses theatrical devices to carry off the disguise. He's a fake.

BREAKING THE SPELL

The deeper truths of this story have much relevance for our present discussion. What was true of the 'Great and Terrible Wizard of Oz' is true of all the other witches and wizards of our experience: they are in fact ordinary human beings with no special powers at all. Notice that there are two ways of seeing the Wizard of Oz: before the screen fell over and afterwards. Before, Dorothy and her friends were in a state of terror and wonderment at the power of this Wizard; miraculous powers are ascribed to him and he is an object of fear and respect. After the screen is removed, however, he is revealed as a rather pathetic old man with no special powers at all. He's a humbug and a fake.

In the 'before' state, we are all (like Dorothy) in childhood, with a child's perceptions and limited understanding of the ways of the world. Those who were the witches and wizards of our childhood were perceived in the same way as Dorothy perceived the Wizard of Oz, 'great and terrible'. They had all the power, and we had very little. They commanded respect and we regarded them as having the power of gods and goddesses. So when did the magic spell that they had placed upon us disappear?

Only when *the screen* was removed. What does this screen represent?

The screen is a barrier, a symbol of the *status quo* and everything that prevents, and stands in the way of, our understanding, insight and awareness. It prevents our maturity and growing up, and forbids us access to the truth that, say, Father Christmas doesn't really exist. The screen acts as a blindfold to how things really are. Truth to tell, sometimes the screen simply falls over, as in The Wizard of Oz. Or we may, through desperation or insight, simply tear it down.

There can be both fear and relief of having broken the biggest taboo we have regarded as sacrosanct, that has the force of a Rule of the Universe: *our parents were human after all*! We fear the discovery of this truth because in some strange way we need their power to protect us and we now wonder if we can survive without it. Yet we are also relieved to know that, in spite of their extravagant claims to be 'great and terrible' and to possess infinite power, they are in fact ordinary mortals.

One of my clients expressed this moment of truth for him as his 'screen' fell over one day in the kitchen of his family home. 'Karl' was only fourteen when it happened. Father had come home in a drunken rage and was removing his belt to administer the usual thrashing:

> *For the first time in my life, I thought, 'He's not going to do this to my mum or me. We've had enough of this.' I went across and grabbed him by the collar – and suddenly I discovered that I was now bigger than my dad, taller in fact by a good few inches. I lifted him off the floor by the scruff of his neck and told him that if ever he laid a finger on my mum or me again, I'd kill him! I let him go, and suddenly my dad fell to the floor, crying and whimpering*

like a dog. From that day on, my dad never laid a finger on us again. Somehow, I think I got his respect.

This young man's screen finally fell over, and his discovery was twofold: Karl came into a knowledge of *his own* power and strength, but also of his father's pathetic nature and intrinsic weakness, the characteristic of every bully ever born. He found, like Dorothy, that this was just an ordinary man, not God Almighty. Life was never going to be the same again.

This moment of truth is always mixed: scary - yet exhilarating. It is the moment of psychological release from the thraldom of childhood – and we know that things can never be the same again. Somehow, we receive insight born perhaps of desperation. The worm finally turns. I find it amusing to think that in *The Wizard of Oz*, it was a small dog that was instrumental in bringing about this change of affairs. A 'dumb animal' was the instrument of truth!

The effect of such a discovery is literally life transforming.

There is no returning to the way things were, or rather how we *thought* they were. It is like crossing the Rubicon: there is no way back, no re-inventing or replacing Father Christmas. The magic of Oz has finally gone. We have abandoned our quest for the magical solution to life.

Yet this discovery is a necessary preliminary to our future growth – like Dorothy and her friends, it made them fall back on their own resources which had lain dormant. They now discovered their new potential. So, the outcome of the unmasking of the Wizard of Oz was two fold:

First, they stopped looking for external, magical solutions to their problems, and secondly, they discovered resources within themselves, which enabled them to lead completely different lives.

This is the practical implementation of all that we have learned. We have finally begun to discard the old wardrobe that was handed down to us by our families; we can now make a personal choice of what we will wear, clothing that is now far more congruent to our new identity and our new way of life.

The Lion, the Witch and the Wardrobe become things of the past. The memory of the harm they have done remains. We cannot expunge it. But their power has been broken. It is the end of childish enslavement.

CHAPTER THREE
Theme: Defences

HOW COULD I PROTECT MYSELF?

The child can emotionally survive only by virtue
of a massive fortification of its psyche.
While such fortifications or psychological defences
are essential to its survival through childhood,
they inevitably distort or compromise
its life as an adult."
[M. S. Peck: 1983, p.130]

The over-riding aim of all organisms is to survive.

This aim is an inherited feature in our evolutionary process. In this respect, humans are no different from the rest of nature. There is an inbuilt survival script imprinted within each one of us as part of our genetic inheritance. It is only by this means that the species may survive, and the urge to do so is essential to all animal and vegetable propagation. In short, Old Mother Nature wants her offspring to survive at least until they have propagated the species, and for humans this means surviving into adulthood.

Survival needs, therefore, form the main thrust of all our

infant motivation. There appears to be no pain that we will not suffer, no conditions that we will not submit to, no conditioning that we will not accept, no humiliations that we will not surrender to – provided thereby we survive. And, truth to tell, we have all developed in this way within our families of origin.

It may be hard for some of us to think our way back to the time when we were very young children. I find it increasingly significant that many adults whom I counselled have no recollection of their childhood whatsoever. Others, knowing something of the pain they suffered at the hands of their families, resist any invitation to examine how it was for them. Some of these have gone so far as to deny their childhood experiences and choose rather to take refuge in an idealisation process. "I had a very happy childhood; there is no point in examining it further!" (Client-speak for "Let's not go there!") These people have adopted the human defence mechanism known as 'denial'. Since these mechanisms are so determinative for our future development it may be useful to examine some of the more familiar of them in this chapter. They will give us clues to our question: How could I protect myself?

SOME HUMAN DEFENCE MECHANISMS

(a) Denial:

This is not the ordinary denial of that which we know to be false. Rather, it involves the warding off from our conscious awareness those facts or memories that may be either totally threatening or merely inconvenient to us. Memories of our childhood that were overwhelming in their intensity of pain may have to be denied in order to keep the pain of those memories at bay. Of course, denial does not remove them; it merely enables us to turn a 'blind eye' to them and treat them as if they had never happened. If we carry, for example, the image of a perfect parent, we must not allow anything to enter our consciousness that may challenge that image. Perhaps we could think of denial as a process of unconsciously lying. It may be healthier for us to maintain the image of an idealised parent rather than abandon this image for the truth of what they were actually like. Better to believe we were loved and nurtured than that we were neglected and abandoned.

(b) Repression:
R. D. Laing's memorable definition of repression is: "*Forgetting, and forgetting that one has forgotten.*" This is the most basic form of human defence, and often lies at the heart of the Everyman's illness of depression. In order to fulfil the supreme goal of infancy, survival, the neonate often represses experiences of deprivation of those resources the lack of which threaten its survival, for fear of wreaking vengeance on the parents on whom it otherwise depends. (This has been amply illustrated by post-war debriefing of prisoners of war where they often collude with their captors; it is known then as 'brainwashing'.) Infantile rage has little chance of acceptance so it must be repressed in the interests of its personal survival. Having repressed the image of the withholding parent, the child may then relate to mother as Mother Earth and father as a Sky God. This defence mechanism is not a conscious, thought-out process; rather, it seems to be an inherited human instinct consistent with survival needs. Its importance is seen when we ask, "What happens to all that repressed material, all those painful memories?" Though buried deeply within us, they are buried *alive*! Things we have forgotten do not simply disappear. It is more like the familiar story of the ostrich burying its head

in the sand. The reality of repressed pain remains real though outside of conscious awareness. Much human energy is needed to keep the lid on our psychological dustbins, and this process is a key element in subsequent experiences of depression. As the word suggests, psychic material is being de-pressed, and to do that we must use up much-needed energy.

Most people who are depressed complain of loss of energy, and of waking up tired. That part of us that knows about our repressed material is working hard to keep it out of our conscious awareness, but this takes a toll on our levels of energy. On those occasions when such material cannot be contained any longer, we experience life-threatening conflict going on within us. When the lid finally blows off, we call this a 'mental breakdown'. What has 'broken down', of course, is our human defence system and this – rather than being perceived as a catastrophe – can in fact be the first step on our road to recovery. Sooner or later, that psychic dustbin needs emptying and the process of counselling or psychotherapy is one method of achieving this in a controlled and caring manner.

(c) Splitting:

Even in the worst cases of child-rearing, some experiences are inevitably thought to be 'good'. In trying to 'make sense' of its world, the child seems to have an ingenious built-in mechanism to account for both the good and the bad things that happen to it. We call it 'splitting'.

It seems that the infant has the capacity to stay in touch with reality by inventing *two* Mothers (or Fathers). There is the Bad Mother who does not come, or touch, or feed the child; and then there is the Good Mother who eventually turns up with at least some resources. The image of the Bad Mother is 'split off' from awareness in order to attend to the Good

Mother. The process of 'splitting' has been well documented by behavioural psychologists, and formed an important part of the research conducted by Ivan Pavlov in the nineteenth century. He discovered that if he withheld food long enough from the dogs on which he experimented, there occurred a "Trans-marginal Stress" which could not be tolerated within the canine system. It may be illustrated thus:

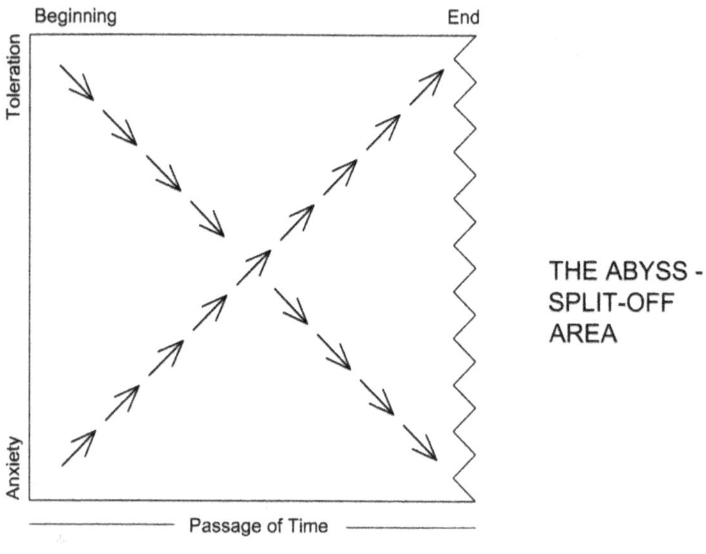

At the commencement of Pavlov's experiments, he found that the dogs possessed *maximum* levels of toleration and *minimum* levels of anxiety. As the waiting time extended, their tolerance began to diminish, while their anxiety levels increased. Eventually, as food was withheld for an intolerable length of time, toleration finally gave out, and anxiety reached alarming, unbearable proportions. Such a process is not capable of being sustained indefinitely; the brain's 'safety mechanism' comes into operation and rescues the sufferer (canine or human) by splitting off the pain from awareness. If this were physical pain, the sufferer would fall into unconsciousness; but as it is mental or psychological pain the splitting-off occurs in the psyche itself. Such split-off pain remains as part of the human unconsciousness, submerged within the depths of the psyche. It can now no longer be remembered as having happened.

However, it continues to form a part of our total world experience. This unutterable and unbearable pain actually scars us for life; and when it occurs in the earliest months of our life, there are actually no words to describe what we have undergone. At best, it emerges as a 'vague' or 'uncomfortable' feeling. Splitting-off such awareness of pain, therefore, is not a conscious decision but part of our autonomic human self-protection kit.

(d) Projection:

If the ramifications of splitting appear rather esoteric, there will be no such risk of misunderstanding the defence known as Projection. The reason is that most of us are engaging in this activity most of the time. In simple terms we may define it as the proverbial pot calling the kettle black.

Richard Nelson-Jones says: *"People tend to project onto others aspects of themselves that they do not find particularly likeable."* [1983, p.105] Its chief characteristic is the disowning of unacceptable feelings and, by projecting such feelings onto others, we are then free to condemn them because they 'belong' to someone else. For instance, if I am angry with you and for some reason I do not find that feeling acceptable to my self-image, then I am free to project that anger onto you, and then say, "You're angry with me!" Or, if I have an intense (subconscious) dislike of myself, I can say to you, "You never have liked me, have you?" It is as if we are addressing a part of *ourselves* under the disguise of talking to another person. This characteristic of human communication is one of the most disruptive forces at work within family relationships. It is ubiquitous because it arises out of its simplicity and ease of use, and – like most defence stratagems – is learnt very early on in our childhood. We want somehow to avoid being blamed for our *actions*, to escape the responsibility, if not the punishment, that might ensue if we were to come clean. We learn - since there are enough unhelpful models around in our families to learn from! - how others escape their responsibilities and we simply follow suit. Escaping the responsibility for our own *feelings*, therefore, is simply an extension of this process.

The sinister consequences of this defence mechanism is found in the assumption that, because whatever happens to be the matter is your fault, then you are responsible for putting things right again! If *my* anger gets projected onto you, then *you* are the one whose behaviour must change. It is your 'act', not mine, that must be 'got together'. I therefore come out of the exchange smelling of roses.

(e) Introjection:

This is the very opposite of projection, and it works by taking something from the environment or from another person and making it my own. If by Projection the 'buck stops *there*', by Introjection the 'buck stops *here*'.

Introjection is like taking on board the expectations, attitudes, assessments and beliefs, which in reality belong to other people. Hence, we grow up trying to be what other people want and expect us to be, regardless of our true ambitions. We inevitably become *Pleasers*. We become a puppet personality rather than a true Self; other people are always somehow pulling our strings.

Herein lies both the danger and the pay-off: the *danger* is that we become ciphers rather than real people; the *pay-off* is that everyone likes us! We may end up with a view of the world that says that the only safe way to be in the world is to be what others want me to be.

The damage done thereby to our selfhood is incalculable. People emerge from this process as clones of others, an amalgam of often contradictory ideas and ideals of other people. The process, because it is largely unaware, never gets challenged rationally. We get into the habit of ingesting the beliefs of other people and end up with not an original thought in our head. The list of 'oughts' and 'shoulds' appear never-ending. We are always carrying an 'under-dog' script around with us, parading our faults like Brownie badges on our sleeves. The over-riding impression we display is, "I'm no good!"

At a practical level, using this defensive stratagem means that we can avoid a really critical look at our world and ourselves. Through introjection, we defend against living in a real world where we must discover who we truly are, choosing to remain a clone of others.

(f) Idealisation:

This defence mechanism combines the use of splitting with projection. There appears to be a need within most infants to retain the 'idea' of the perfect, all-supplying parents. After all, it might be catastrophic to consider the idea of a universe governed completely by chance. (Indeed, Sigmund Freud posited the origins of religious faith in God arising from this need to ward off such a potential catastrophe and was *'born from man's need to make his helplessness tolerable..'* [1961, p.23]

In spite of all the evidence to the contrary, therefore, the infant wills to retain the idea of the perfection and unbounded resources of its parents. It does this by splitting-off all evidence to the contrary – the bad experiences – and projecting onto the parent-figures all that is good. The infant ends up with the 'idea' of perfect parents intact, but at the expense of truth.

Much of the work done in marital therapy involves the unlearning of such defensive strategies. The need (in the infant) for the perfect parent, re-emerges in the life of the male adult for the perfect wife and in the female for the perfect husband. Neither is a realistic hope! While the mature adult can sustain imperfections in a partner, a 'child' cannot. Hence, immature adults retain their need for a 'perfect parent' intact and bring it unconsciously into their adult partnerships. By 'idealising' (idolising?) other people we create a world of illusion, where everything is 'just perfect'. It is, in fact, merely a fool's paradise. We live in a world belonging to *Pollyanna*.

Adult maturity is measured by the amount of imperfection we can tolerate in our world, our own as well as that of other people.

(g) Reaction Formation:
The basis of this defence is that I hide one emotion, or part of my awareness, by another, more acceptable one. For example, Freud maintained that this defensive stratagem was an activity of the Super-Ego (or Super Self) keeping out of our awareness (and thus our behaviour) unacceptable parts of our thinking or behaving. The essence of the way this defence works is seen in the formation of a reaction totally at variance with what actually happens to be the truth at the time. If we should be faced, for instance, with a pornographic picture to which part of our *mind* would like to say, "Wow!", through Reaction Formation what would come out of our *mouth* would be, "Ugh! How disgusting!" The instinctive part of us (or what Freud called our Id) is immediately crushed by the condemning part of us (our Super

Ego) so that in time most of our responses are about 180 degrees from the real truth. Dr. Frank Lake lists some of the more easily recognised patterns of Reaction Formation thus:

The Repressed Activity	***Reactive pattern of behaviour***
Attention-seeking fantasies are a defence when mental pain is caused by the failure of the source-person to pay attention.	*Excessive self-effacement. This gives the impression that one does not wish to attract attention. Shyness and blushing express this conflict.*
Rage and destructiveness. Fantasies of compelling the mother and father to fall in with the will of the infant, which in fantasy is omnipotent. The super-ego has compelled the raging ego to turn the rage back on itself.	*The compulsive compliant personality is the answer in consciousness. Contradicting the inner desire to dominate and compel the parental figures, the reaction pattern is of submission and willingness to be controlled.*
Despair of the mother ever responding to the infant's need still reverberates in the memory. Hope is almost extinguished. Expectation of help has almost faded. All this has to be denied.	*Compulsive optimism and persistence. He refuses to admit defeat. Though despondent, he persists in flogging himself, in the vain hope that he will make the grade by his own efforts.*
Worthlessness. If nobody bothers to answer the intense longing of the infant for life, by coming to it, this devalues the self to the point of annihilation.	*Compulsive striving to achieve worth and value. He has a compulsive need to be needed. Tends to take on too many key jobs.*

[1986, pp.45-49]

In a simple kind of way, Reaction Formation is a subtle form of denial. Only we don't know that we are denying what is really true about our thoughts and feelings.

(h) Rationalisation:
This form of defence operates by denying that we are defending! In its most classic form, rationalisation is a form of Super-Denial and would have others (and ourselves) believe that things really *are* how they appear. Any system of defence that denies its existence is a most subtle form of behaviour. This gives Rationalisation its deadly power.

Rationalisation works by giving an excuse for behaviour that sounds entirely logical. When confronted by any inconsistency, the person using this defence mechanism always has a reason. Their catchphrase is, "Oh, that's only because..." One woman I recall using this system to defend herself tried to convince me that our differences in understanding her presenting problem were due to my being biased in her favour! Sometimes people will say you are 'too kind' or 'too optimistic' or even that 'you need glasses', in order to maintain their poor self-image. They have become convinced that they are ugly or worthless and any voice that appears to contradict their way of perceiving themselves is dismissed as 'being kind' or even 'being untruthful': 'You're only saying that....'

A man I once met had been treated abominably by his parents, but he defended his parents by saying that, "I was probably a bit of a handful!" When I persisted that they appeared to have used undue violence against him, he replied, "They meant well!" Pursuing my attempt to help him see his history in a different light I volunteered the thought that as a father, he would not treat his children in that way. He smiled and said, "Ah, but I lack the wisdom my parents had!" By this time my own frustration told me I was barking up the wrong tree, and that his rationalisation was probably holding him together. To defend oneself by denying one is defending is a very hard barrier to breach.

THE DESTRUCTIVE EFFECT OF UNCONSCIOUS DEFENCE MECHANISMS

It is important at this point to explain that it is not wrong to defend ourselves. As I said earlier, this is an innate part of our biological evolution and necessary to our survival. In all of the above Defence Mechanisms it is true to say that they came into being in order to help the person survive their environment, usually as very young children. But Defence Mechanisms that are totally unconscious are dangerous simply because we have to use up so much energy to keep them in place. Having adopted them in order to survive, the healthy thing to do is to discard them when the perceived danger is past. But since most of us do not know that we are defended, little attempt is made to discard them. We have come to believe that their effect is 'simply me' and that is how I have to come to terms with myself. This is what I call 'Maginot Line Thinking'.

Maginot Line Thinking:
Prior to the 1939-1945 War, an elaborate defensive barrier was constructed in Northeast France at the instigation of the then French War Minister, Andre Maginot. It was intended as a fortification against German invasion. Its purpose was doubtless laudable, given the continuing threat from the German Third Reich. The Maginot Line was much more sophisticated than the Berlin Wall; it had living quarters and

air-conditioned facilities for the troops. Although it covered the Franco-German border adequately, it stopped at the Belgian frontier.

In May, 1940, the German army invaded Belgium, and, outflanking the impregnable Maginot Line, marched on into France making the French defence system redundant. Since the French guns were cemented in place, facing Germany, they could not even be turned around to fire on the invading troops behind the French fortification.

There is, at least in my opinion, a direct analogy here with all human systems of *psychological* defence. Erected at a time of real threat, they are workable systems in the war of survival; but once the theatre of war has moved on, the old systems of defence are useless.

"Maginot Line Thinking" might represent a rather potty French colonel who, in 1944, still mans the Maginot Line defences looking northward for the expected German invasion! The Maginot Line is now an object of military history, a tourist attraction, a curiosity, and a memorial to an obsolete form of defence. Most of our own human forms of defence are likewise obsolete. They were erected at a time of extreme danger and in the face of a very real threat to our survival; and to that extent they worked. Our denial, or projection, or introjection was adopted in the face of overwhelming odds when annihilation appeared to be the alternative to having no defences at all. The repression or splitting or reaction formation all came to our aid in the light of the overwhelming forces facing us at the time, and their effectiveness is seen in the fact that we are alive to tell the tale. To the infant, halitosis is better than no breath at all!

So far, so good.

But human defences, once they have served their purpose, need to be dismantled. Unfortunately, most of us survive into adulthood with our childhood defences intact. We do not take account of the change in our circumstances now as adults; we carry with us a small, vulnerable and threatened child within us that still cries out for protection against the formidable forces of its parents or parental substitutes. This is no longer necessary, especially in those cases where the child's parents are now dead! Laughing at my picture of that potty French colonel still keeping watch in his Maginot bunker, we may not perhaps see the ludicrous situation we ourselves are in by doing precisely the same thing! Of course, one case is visible and material, the other is invisible and psychological; nevertheless, I believe that this is one of the major causes of human distress and pain. A defended Self, when the need for such defence is long past, leads to a denied, devalued Self. We are not who we think we are. [See further my article, 1994.]

COPING WITH OUR UNACCEPTABILITY

The message that many us of received very early on in our experience of life – if not within the womb itself – was that we were unacceptable. Believing naturally, as most infants do, that its parents were God-like, who were we to argue with them? The origin of such infant thinking lies far back in the Greek legends of the gods; if they were not pleased, punishment – often arbitrary and severe – would ensue. Every newborn infant comes into the world with the Greek Legend firmly fixed in its unconscious memories, among what Carl Jung called "archetypes". Parents, by definition, are incontrovertible and always right!

Rather than consider that it might – just might, mind you – be thought that our parents have got it wrong, it is easier and far safer to surrender, and believe that it is we who have got things all wrong. If our parents are punishing us, then, according to the archetypal myth deeply buried within us, we must deserve it.

It does not seem to matter that we cannot find any reason for the punishment or deprivation meted out to us. If it is happening, then it must be for a purpose and therefore we must bow to it and accept it. This is the way we begin to deny ourselves and commence the systematic protection of our vulnerable selves by adopting some of the defence mechanisms I have briefly outlined above.

Dr. Susan Forward writes:

> *When we're young, our godlike parents are everything to us. Without them, we would be unloved, unprotected, unhoused and unfed, living in a constant state of terror, knowing we were unable to survive alone. They are all-powerful providers. We need, they supply.*
>
> *With nothing and no one to judge them against, we assume them to be perfect parents...The child is at the mercy of his godlike parents and, like the ancient Greeks, never knows when the next lightning bolt will strike. But the child of toxic parents knows that the lightning is coming sooner or later. This fear becomes deeply ingrained and grows with the child. At the core of every formerly mistreated adult – even high achievers – is a little child who feels powerless and afraid.* [1989, p.15ff.]

If the early message that many of us received was, "You're no good!", it is not surprising that we grow up with this lie intact. Defending against the conflict of maintaining both a Good Self-image and a Bad Self-image, most of us capitulate to the idea, ingrained in us for years, that our parents are right and that we are bad, unacceptable, unless we conform to their conditions and stipulations. Through defence mechanisms, therefore, we learn to deny the original good part of us in order to survive. Having repressed our early sense of goodness, we have now forgotten that we have forgotten! Our primal need to survive and to find some form of acceptance is so strong that we will do literally anything to achieve it. In so doing, we incur enormous psychological damage, which often takes years of psychotherapy to rectify. Alas, in some cases, the child does not survive that long.

In a widely reported case of child abuse, one little girl was deprived not only of affection and basic care but also of sufficient food to survive. She was kept locked in a small room, with a urine-sodden mattress her only solace. When she called out to be fed, her father would enter the room and thrash her. She learned not to call out even though she was starving. When she was eventually found dead in the small, locked room, she had massive injuries, and a post-mortem discovered her stomach filled with wallpaper which she had chosen to eat to assuage her hunger rather than offend her father by demanding food.

Such stories have the power to reach most of us deeply, and to trigger off feelings of revulsion, rage and pity. What strikes me forcefully as I recall such a tragic story is that, rather than go against her father's wishes, she would eat the wallpaper instead. Choosing which way to die is never easy, and not always conscious, as in this awful case. Yet, in a strange way, this young child chose to die rather than contravene her parents' wishes. Such is the godlike power they possess to small and vulnerable children, as Dr. Forward makes abundantly clear.

Thankfully, such extreme cases as this are rare. Yet for our purposes here, it illustrates most poignantly the power that parents possess in any young child's experience. This young child's self-denial issued in her death, but for many others it issues in the death of the spirit, a kind of *psychological* death that is masked by a living body that contains, like a sepulchre, the ghastly experience of abandonment.

The method of self-defence that operates by denying any method of self-defence results in the most serious form of self-delusion. Perhaps this is why I often shiver when my clients told me of their 'perfect childhood' when the facts they present seem to deny any such perfection. Of course, parents – and I am one of them – are on a hiding to nothing: if our children turn out OK it is due solely to their own efforts; if not, it's all our fault! Parents seemingly can't win. Yet, there is a wide gap between the 'good enough parents' we try to be and the form of parenthood that can only operate by the total extinction of any semblance of individuality in their children.

In the battle of the will, the Lions usually win.

Parents who can only rule by force and violence do untold damage to their offspring. I began this chapter by quoting Michael Peck: "The child can emotionally survive only by virtue of a massive fortification of its psyche." But children – all of us – have paid a high price for this survival.

This phenomenon came home to me forcefully when I was watching that supreme mime artist, Marcel Marceau, in one of his famous sketches. He goes out into his garden one day where the flowers bloom and the sun shines, and everything seems wonderful. But he sees a crisp packet that has blown into his garden, and he decides to build a low brick wall in order to keep offending objects from spoiling his view. The next day there are two crisp packets, so he builds the wall still higher. Each day there is more litter invading his garden, and so the wall gets higher and higher. One day, he goes out into his garden and – at last! – there is no litter anywhere. His garden is litter-free - but all his flowers are dead from lack of sunlight, and there are no birds singing.

It seems to me that this story is one that many people can apply to themselves; they have needed to incorporate defence mechanisms (brick walls) into their lives, to keep at bay those forces (the emotional litter) that would spoil their lives, but those very defences often keep out the sunlight, which may stand for happiness, contentment and enjoyment. Our human energy resources are spent in 'fire-watching' rather than in creative enjoyment. So familiar do these circumstances become that we somehow fall into a reluctant acceptance of them and abandon any hope that life could be any different. There seems to be no other way to cope with our innate sense of unacceptability.

The American writer, Henry David Thoreau, once said that "the mass of men live lives of quiet desperation". On good days, such desperation is kept just beneath the surface, but stays within us as a generalised torpor, a sense of unease, a niggling sense that all is not well within. Many people cannot even find words for what they feel, and settle for a shrug or a frown, or a "y'know". The need now is for us to start to make connections.

MAKING CONNECTIONS

Elizabeth Noble in her helpful book *Primal Connections* [1993] says:

> *Making connections is the goal and the reward of these inner journeys. It is the experience of re-associating and reorganizing feelings and state-dependent memories that*

> *lead us to resolution, not just the reliving. Activating resources that were originally denied and utilizing new choices are the keys to empowerment...making connections is like finding lost treasures.* [p.120f.]

It would repay the effort for you to go back over periods and experiences in your own life, in particular the origins and sources of your system of belief about life, yourself and others, and try to identify where they originated. Look at what you believe about yourself (as opposed to what you may tell other people), about what is right and what is wrong (morals and ethics), about religious beliefs (spirituality) and ask yourself how you came by this knowledge. Chances are you may find yourself having gone through life on a psychological 'auto-pilot', being guided through life by a navigational setting determined by someone else.

We may even ask ourselves why we have allowed such a state of affairs to have continued for so long. The chief reason is twofold: first, it's easier to blame someone else for the state of our lives; and, secondly, if we choose to come off 'auto-pilot' we have to take responsibility for our own selves.

Our previous examples have shown how such choices can only be madc once we have begun to make connections, between the relationship of our *present* existence and our *past* conditioning. "So this is why….."

Marie Cardinal, admittedly through a prolonged period of psychoanalysis, eventually made the connection between her own suicidal feelings and the death wish of her mother. Marie's 'need to die' was connected to mother's wish for her death (an intended abortion).

During my own therapy, I made a number of important connections, between chronic feelings of inferiority and the mask of assurance that I often wore. I made a connection between the doctor's opinion that I was 'in the wrong' and the way this had propelled me through life trying to prove that I was 'in the right'.

Ross Connelly made the connection between her own chronic feelings of abandonment by her mother, and the historical transfer of her mother's sexual role with her husband to that of her daughter. Her feelings were totally vindicated.

Graham Farrant [p.7] made the connection between his persistent feelings of 'of being not wanted', of feeling abandoned, and his mother's actions in trying to attain an abortion.

The importance of making such connections is: *in order that we may disconnect from their potentially lethal power.* In almost every case, we will find some kind of *vindication* of our feelings, so often in the past dismissed as 'me being silly' or, 'I suppose I've got that all wrong!" There is always a part of our true selves that is the repository of truth, residing on the 'hard disc' in our psychic memory that records our experiences of our 'primal pain'. This 'still small voice' may be hidden under layers of conditioning and defence mechanisms, but it is never totally erased. When we finally give it permission to speak, a reality emerges that can be both frightening and almost unbelievable, but yet a reality that is somehow recognised as familiar and true.

William Shakespeare somehow knew all this when he wrote:

To thine own self be true.

In the following chapter we shall go on to examine how our human defences reveal themselves in the many disguises we end up wearing in our adult life.

CHAPTER FOUR
Theme: Disguises

THE MAN IN THE IRON MASK

'A man without a mask' is indeed very rare.
One even doubts the possibility of such a man.
Everyone in some measure wears a mask,
and there are many things we do not put ourselves into fully.
In 'ordinary' life it seems hardly possible
for it to be otherwise.
[R. D. Laing: 1965, p.95]

Which of us is not aware of hiding behind a mask on occasions, of concealing our true identity and feelings? Must we not agree with the truth of Ronnie Laing's words quoted above? The theme of this chapter is the subject of his important book, *The Divided Self*. The ideas of 'mask' and 'division' are not so very far apart. One results in the other.

In 1848, the French writer Alexandre Dumas wrote a book whose title in English became *The Man in the Iron Mask*. It has since been made into a number of screen epics.

The 'man' in question has never been identified with any certainty, but he was almost undoubtedly a political prisoner incarcerated by Louis XIV in the Bastille where he died in 1703.

However, the title is a very suggestive one when we come to examine the subject of human personality, since we could use it analogically with a certain degree of accuracy to describe how many of us live most of the time.

Perhaps the most obvious comparison to note is that a mask acts as both *pretence* and *concealment,* and acts as a dividing line between outer and inner realities. When children dress in Guy Fawkes masks on bonfire night, they are taking part in an elaborate disguise whose rules are open for all to see. It is not really Guy Fawkes who is standing there with his pathetic attempt to recreate the 'guy' for whom pennies are demanded. It is really little Johnny, whose reality will be revealed when his mother can finally coax him into the bath. But for the moment, Johnny can be permitted to 'become' someone else, as all Fancy Dress parties allow us to do. Such play-acting is harmless enough – necessary, even – because everyone knows the rules of 'let's pretend' and no-one is seriously trying to fool anyone else into believing that they really are the person their mask suggests.

PSYCHOLOGICAL MASKS

Psychological masks, however, are rather more sinister. The division between the outer and inner realities is not so easy to discover. Everyone – including the wearer – believes that 'what you see is what you get'. This is far from the truth, as we shall now discover.

We noticed in the previous chapter how, through the long process of defensive behaviour, we have had to deny aspects of our essential self. The purpose was, as we noticed, survival. The serious result of such necessary defensive behaviour is that there is now a division between our inner and outer selves. Like the Man in the Iron Mask, we are imprisoned behind a façade. The split is often just below the surface of our awareness.

For example, there is in common language a way of talking about this division. We say, "Well, a bit of me wants this, but another bit wants that!" Concerning some decision we are trying to make we may say, "My head knows what I ought to do but my heart is not in it!" In fact, we speak like this most of the time concerning our difficulty in making decisions, expressing preferences, sharing emotions or making choices. We know, instinctively, that our selves are divided, split up between often-warring factions within us. It is frequently by such conflict that we become aware of our divided selves. We find ourselves admitting that we find it hard to reconcile some intended action with who we are. "I don't know what came over me!" Or, after a time of ill health, we may say, "I'm feeling my old self again."

Such is the complexity of the situation that, before going any further, we must grasp the nettle and ask the important question which has bedevilled discussion on the nature of human personality: What exactly *is* the Self?

THE NATURE OF THE SELF

In the very broadest of terms, answers to our question appear to revolve around the use – and, of supreme importance, the *meaning* – of language. Where do begin to define The Self? It is not enough to say, simply, my Self is me. For then we have to go on to ask, Who am I? Ken Wilber gives us a place to start:

> *Who am I? The query has probably tormented mankind since the dawn of civilization, and remains today one of the most vexing of all human questions. Answers have been offered which range from the sacred to the profane, the complex to the simple, the scientific to the romantic, the political to the individual... Yet there is an even more basic process underlying the whole procedure of establishing an identity. Something very simple happens when you answer the question, 'Who are you?' When you are describing or explaining or even just inwardly feeling your 'self', what you are actually doing, whether you know it or not, is drawing a mental line or boundary across the whole field of your experience, and everything on the* inside *of that boundary you are feeling or calling your 'self', while everything* outside *that boundary you feel to be 'not-self'. Your self-identity, in other words, depends entirely upon where you draw that boundary line.* [1985, p.4.]

Wilber goes on to remind us that a complicating factor consists in the fact that this boundary line can, and frequently does, shift. It can be re-drawn, and indeed needs to be re-drawn as we discover both hidden parts of the self that we have hitherto been unaware of or denied, and – most important of all – parts that belong to the outside (especially to other people and their influences) and are in fact no part of our Self at all. Every time we go through what we may call 'an identity crisis' this is the process in which we are taking part. We are in a period of re-assessment of where the boundary is.

THREE CASE STUDIES

The Story of William

"William" arrived to see me one day in a bit of a lather. He was flushed, and rather breathless. "Something awful has happened!" he gasped. "I can't believe it!" Eventually, he went on to tell me about a row between him and his wife, during the course of which he had slapped her around the face. "That's not me!" he told me vehemently. I reminded him of what he had just said, and that he had admitted to me that it was indeed him who had hit his wife. His problem was admitting it to himself. What did he mean by such a denial? Psychologically, two things were happening that he could not reconcile.

First, some activity that he had previously considered to be part of the *external* world (to use Wilber's metaphor), that is, where men hit their wives, was discovered to be on the *inside*! Second, he was in the process of questioning the boundary between the internal and external worlds. I reminded him that although the man who had hit his wife was 'him', it was a part of 'William' he had never previously encountered. He had stumbled across an undiscovered part of his self-image, a potential for violence, which prior to this incident he had never imagined was part of him. He needed to revise his self-image, to re-draw the boundary, so that he could now see himself as quite capable of violence when the circumstances were present to do so (in this case his wife's confession to an affair with the gardener.) Such a revision of self-image is indeed an 'identity crisis'. In his case, William had never before considered himself to be capable of such behaviour. It can be a frightening thing to encounter previously unknown parts of the Self – which Carl Jung named 'the Shadow' – especially when they emerge in the form of physical violence. No wonder we try to disown them as 'Not-me'.

Another case concerns a slightly different issue, not violence but sexual orientation.

The Story of Euan

"Euan" had been having homosexual fantasies ever since his adolescence. Only once had they been acted out, in a public toilet where he and an older man had engaged in mutual masturbation. Here is an example of a man with a quite conscious 'inner reality' but which he had spent years trying to push outside himself, to disown, to be part of the great 'Not-me'. In Euan's case, his latent homosexuality was totally inimical to his more acceptable self-concept as heterosexually oriented. Dynamically, by maintaining such latent feelings as 'Not-me', he was using the psychological defence known as Repression. Rather than removing the conflict, repression merely pushes it further underground.

By a long process of therapy, Euan was eventually helped to retrieve this hidden part of himself and to accept it into his conscious self-concept. He was still consciously and actively heterosexual but now he could accept, in line with the findings of the Kinsey Report, that introduced a scale of sexual preferences from 1 – 7, that at least a small part of him was capable of attraction to other men. By moving from denial to acceptance, Euan could enlarge his self-concept to include what previously had been a totally *un*acceptable part of himself. He could abandon The Man in the Iron Mask 'act' and, in this regard at least, become less divided than hitherto. The importance of such a move (enlargement of self-concept) is that he was now aware of this aspect of his sexuality and it was this awareness and acceptance that gave him power over it: to choose to act on it or not.

The late Virginia Satir comments wisely,

> *...you probably have many parts that you have not yet discovered. All these parts, whether you have owned them or not, are present in you. Becoming aware of them enables you to take charge of them rather than be enslaved by them. Each of your parts is a vital source of energy.* [Quoted in John Rowan, 1990, p.103]

John Rowan sums up what appears to be a universal rule:

> ***"I cannot manage anything I do not own."***

By owning, to himself and to his therapist, that there was a latent homosexuality within him, Euan was able to release the energy he was using to repress that awareness, and divert it into 'managing' this part of him. He was now back in control of his feelings.

The Story of Hungerford

Out of a clear blue sky on the morning of Wednesday, 19th August, 1987, a young man named Michael Ryan left his house in the small market town of Hungerford in Berkshire. He was dressed in battle fatigues, and appeared in the guise of a character, John Rambo, made famous by the film *Rambo*, starring Sylvester Stallone. He was armed to the teeth.

In the course of that fateful day, he wandered around the quiet town, shooting dead sixteen people at random, including his own mother, and later – when finally holed up in the local school by the police – himself. The event shocked the nation and its shockwaves reverberated around the world.

The *Daily Mirror* ran the headline, *The Rambo Killings*. It was the impersonal, random, choice of his victims that made many people question the state of mind of Michael Ryan. He had hitherto been regarded as a bit of a loner, single, living with his mother, and who was a member of the local gun club. What made him go on this homicidal rampage? Answers and suggestions were not slow in coming forward, from blaming his indulgence in the game of Dungeons and Dragons to an acute form of paranoid schizophrenia. We will, of course, never know why Ryan acted as he did. But, somehow, we can say with certainty that something that was growing inside him, be it power-fantasies or a suppressed ego, suddenly broke out in a hideous form. Reality and fantasy became blurred and, if he were suffering from an acute form of paranoid schizophrenia, the voices in his head would have done the rest.

Emotions, together with fantasies of grandeur and the armaments to accompany them, can combine to make a lethal cocktail. The pressure builds up, rather like steam in a kettle, and if it has no natural outlet there is an explosion. Perhaps something like this exploded within the psyche of Michael Ryan. Any single emotion – be it envy, rage, lust – can build up and assume terrifying proportions. Denial may work for a time but if the urge is greater than our defensive ability to contain it, it bursts forth in an uncontrollable way.

William, Euan and Ryan are but three examples of acting 'out of character'. The danger appears to be when we get into a kind of 'either/or' frame of reference regarding our self-image. A healthier image seems to be one that can be 'both/and' – admitting that at least, as a human being, there is nothing of which human beings are capable that will exclude me! When people define themselves in tight, black-and-white, imagery I fear for them. ("Always this…Never that!") They do not seem to make any allowance for circumstances that may be so powerful as to tip them over the edge of their assumed self-identity and then the mask slips.

In William's case, it was the vicious, humiliating disclosure that his wife had been carrying on an affair both under his own roof and also under his own nose. In Euan's case, it was a question of slight inebriation, when his defences were already shaky, and the sight of a man's engorged penis in a public lavatory. In Michael Ryan's case, who knows? There is a strong suggestion that he intended to rape his first victim, Sue, and his inability to do so could have caused an unacceptable level of humiliation and powerlessness, to be compensated for by his arsenal of weapons. It is tempting, and entirely speculative, to wonder whether his ineffective sexual organ, his 'weapon', was transformed into actual weapons that would be seen to 'work'! In any case, Rowan's dictum is paramount: *I cannot manage anything I do not own.*

MODELS OF THE COMPLEXITY OF THE SELF

In order to cut the Gordian knot, we must discard any simplistic notion that there is some inner Real Self that has become corrupted through, for instance, the defensive behaviour outlined in our previous chapter. Such an idea, though simple and attractive, does not begin to do justice to the complexity of human personality. In other words, human personality is divided by nature, and is, in its very consistency, complex.

What do I mean by 'divided by nature'? To start with (as we noticed in Chapter One) the genetic make-up is found to consist of twenty-three chromosomes inherited from each of our parents. Complexity, therefore, appears to be in the very nature of the Self, more especially as we notice what happens when a sperm penetrates the ovum and the genetic multiplication begins to take place. This combination of the contribution by both our parents gives us the clue to the nature of human personality: it is complex, not simple; it is divided, not indivisible; it consists of different parts ("Oh! he gets his temper from his dad but his blue eyes from me!") We must, if we are to make sense of The Self at all, abandon the attractive idea that we are really like the statue in the garden after a fall of snow: if only we could sweep the snow away, the real self would emerge! We need a model of The Self that does justice to the complexity – indeed the dynamic quality – of its nature while at the same time staying within non-technical language.

Whatever model finally emerges (and there are several attractive models on offer) it seems to me vital that we build into our model some form of dynamic structure, capable of doing justice to our capacity for change and growth. This is where the garden statue model falls down: we are not static beings, but dynamic, capable of movement and change.

Several writers have drawn attention to this rather obvious truth. For instance, George Herbert, the seventeenth century poet, wrote:

Oh, what a thing is man! How far from power,
From set'led peace and rest!
He is some twenty sev'ral men at least
Each sev'ral hour.

The English writer, W. Somerset Maugham, says:

There are times when I look over the various parts of my character with perplexity. I recognise that I am made up of several persons and that the person that at the moment has the upper hand will inevitably give place to another.

> *But which is the real one? All of them or none?* [Quoted in Thomas Harris, 1970, p.1]

Further back, in the New Testament, St. Paul bemoans his fate:

> *I do not understand my own actions. For I do not do what I want, but I do the very thing that I hate...I can will what is right, but I cannot do it.* [Romans 7. 15, 18.]

Pioneers of the nineteenth-century discoveries in psychology reflected this conflict. Sigmund Freud introduced a model of human personality that was tripartite: Ego, Super-Ego, and Id. New and often bewildering names began to appear in the vocabulary of psychology to describe the complexity of the Self. All agreed, however, that we were not a simple unity, indivisible and static. There was a dynamic at the very heart of the human Self out of which conflict many of the diagnosable illnesses were said to arise. Freud's three-fold understanding of the basic components of the human personality has never been seriously challenged. The older Body/Mind/Spirit model also comprised a human trinity.

Other, more modern, writers have struggled to describe the complex nature of The Self. Each one of them begins with a simple Inner/Outer division, like the Man in the Iron Mask:

Writer	**Inner**	**Outer**
C. G. Jung	Self	Persona
F. S. Perls	Self	Self-Image
D. Winnicott	True Self	False Self
R. D. Laing	Real Self	False Self

A. Janov	Real Self	Unreal Self
P. Tournier	Person	Persona

John Rowan (who gives a fuller list of divisions in his most helpful *The Reality Game*, 1983, p.58) goes on to remark:

> *What all these investigators are saying is that the ordinary ego, which is presented to the world, and which other people know us by, is false. It is a made-up thing, a mask, a fiction. We may have spent many years building it up, and have invested a lot of energy in it, but it is unreal...It essentially arises out of an attempt to protect the real self from pain.*

His diagram illustrates this by using three concentric circles:

> *Outer Circle: = Positive but phoney*
> *Inner Circle: = Negative Self-image*
> *Centre Circle: = The Self who you really are*

In this model, Rowan points to an essential truth about human beings: we have all been hurt by our past, our identity has been shaped by that hurt, and that we are (often unconsciously) covering up in order to present a positive image of ourselves to the world. That most of us continue in our masquerade is not surprising, considering our options. Rowan lists these as:

(a) "If they knew how nasty (evil, bad, horrible, hating) I really am, they would all hate me;"
(b) "If they knew how inadequate (weak, worthless, inept) I really am, they would all reject me;"
(c) "If they knew how needy (insatiable, sucking in and then

> destroying, attracting and then devouring) I really am, they would all avoid me." [*op.cit.*. p.60]

Rowan correctly perceives these as the authentic voices of the False Self, and thus contributes to the reason for the 'Positive but phoney' outward appearance we assume – our masks. We dare not let people see us as we perceive ourselves: the (mistaken) reason being that we would be hated, rejected and avoided.

So most of us find ourselves caught between the devil and the deep blue sea. We either have to put on a mask of a phoney, positive image, or we risk rejection if we reveal our deeper, negative, self-image. What we do not see – and what all therapeutic interventions are designed to help us to see – is that there is a deeper, truer, self: the real me, my inner core, call it what you will. It is this Self that all humanistic interpretations of human nature (and some interpretations of the Christian story) would see as basically good, a truth that was denied perhaps during our upbringing.

When we speak, therefore, of the 'divided self' we need to notice that there are two different ways in which we can interpret that language. First, we may see it as referring to the basic complexity of human nature itself; or we can see it (as Rowan comments above) as referring to the way in which we have been conditioned during childhood to deny our essential goodness, adopt a negative self-image from our image-makers (as we noticed in Chapter Two) and then end up (in Rowan's outer circle) so defended that we need to masquerade in a positive outfit in order to hide what, by this time, we have come to believe is a thoroughly nasty, negative, worthless person.

An additional aid to understanding these various models of personality is found in the concepts of Gestalt Psychology. *Gestalt* comes from a German word the nearest translation into

English being *pattern* or *shape*. The practice of Gestalt Therapy consists, chiefly, in changing our perspective, seeing new shapes, new possibilities, new aspirations. Its main focus centres upon *awareness*. Its three main concerns consist of (a) I-Thou; (b) Here and now; (c) Not Why but How.

(a) helps us to relate directly, not dealing with anything or anyone outside the intimacy of our meeting;
(b) insists that we keep our thoughts, feelings, words in the immediate here-and-now;
(c) gets away from the incessant 'answers to questions' and deals rather with how things occur, our feelings and our reactions to them.

In terms of understanding our 'divided self' here is a helpful model directly related to stories such as those of William, Euan and Michael Ryan above. It deals with the so-called contradictions within each of us and the conflict that arises from them. It also addresses directly the issue of the personal attitude that maintains: "Always this; never that".

We may call these 'contradictions' *polarities* – indicating that we all contain polar forces, popularly thought to be opposites; for example, we have all expressed the characteristic *kindness*, but also the characteristic of *cruelty*. We can be *both* kind *and* cruel, depending on the circumstances. The healthy person is the one who is most aware of *and owns* these polarities; the unhealthy person is the one who denies the possibility of them – "I'm always this, never that!" Joseph Zinker writes:

The healthy person may not always approve of all his polarities, but the fact that he is willing to suffer their awareness is a significant aspect of his inner strength. There are massive holes in the awareness of a disturbed person. He has a rigid, stereotyped view of himself and is not able to accept many parts of himself; his stinginess, homosexuality, insensitivity, hardness. He denies his so-called negative polarities – those aspects of himself which he has been conditioned to think of as unacceptable or repulsive, and tends to project these characteristics on to others. Becoming aware of these unacceptable polarities makes him anxious. The result is the emergence of neurotic symptoms, with neurosis being the failure to control the emergence of anxiety. [1977, p.200]

It is far healthier to incorporate our polarities into our self-awareness than to deny and reject them. We may not especially like 'the other side' of us, but remember the wisdom of John Rowan: *I cannot manage anything I do not own.* Psychologist Carl Jung named this aspect of the Self as 'the Shadow' but it is not in itself the repository of evil or 'our dark side' alone. The 'Shadow' may contain much that is good and creative (often our sexuality) but which we have been taught to suppress in order to gain the approval of others.

If we deny the possibility of our being, say, cruel we run the risk of cruelty getting 'out of control'. Here we see the insidious outcome of our previous conditioning, whereby we were taught that our acceptability depended upon being 'only this, never that'. Such denial means that our capacity to be cruel, since it 'does not exist', is not within our self-concept and is 'no part of me'. The devastating result of such denial is all around us. William did not accept 'wife-beating' as a possibility within his own self-image, hence when it broke out one day (granted, under provocation) he said, "I don't know what came over me!" What came over him ('overcame him') was his Shadow. These words are often spoken with amazement and shame when behaviour we had hitherto thought of as belonging to *them*, 'out there', suddenly and undeniably becomes part of *me*, 'in here'. Euan did not accept that homosexual attraction belonged to his self-image, and when he eventually succumbed to his encounter, again, something that he thought had belonged 'out there' was discovered 'in here'. Even in the face of the evidence to the contrary, people will still want to maintain that 'that was not me'. Painfully, it was. It was the part of 'me' that I had buried, but buried *alive*! We are not, however, the helpless victims of our 'Shadow side' unless we continue to hide behind our mask of probity and self-delusion. It is healthier to admit, at least to oneself if to no other person, that we do possess the capacity for, say, cruelty or violence or lust; but in our case, by owning it, we can manage it more successfully.

THE CHRISTIAN NEUROSIS

The word we sometimes use to describe a person who does not live up to their self-image, and in whom there is clearly a credibility gap between what they profess and what they perform, is 'hypocrite'. It is a word with an interesting pedigree.

The Greek word υποκριτης was employed to denote a 'stage- or play-actor', or one who answers behind a mask. The hypocrite is one who says one thing but does another. His words and actions do not compute.

I find it a curious anomaly that within his ministry, Jesus of Nazareth spoke out against hypocrisy more than any other human failing. Among the many failings he could have chosen, this one came in for special condemnation. At least in his mind, play-acting was a cardinal sin. The obverse of this truth is that Jesus was concerned for us to become real and genuine. The focus for much of his vitriolic condemnation was upon the religious leaders of his day. For example:

> *"Then said Jesus to the crowds and to his disciples, 'The scribes and the Pharisees sit on Moses' seat; so practice and observe whatever they tell you, but not what they do; for they preach, but do not practice. They bind heavy burdens, hard to bear, and lay them on men's shoulders; but they themselves will not move them with their finger. They do all their deeds to seen by men... Woe to you, scribes and Pharisees, hypocrites!"* [Matthew 23: 1-4; 13.]

In popular parlance hypocrites are called 'two-faced'. It is not an inaccurate description. "False face must hide what the false heart doth know." (Shakespeare's Macbeth).

It is the particular focus and aim of counselling and psychotherapy to work towards the healing of all this damage and duplicity. But its widespread nature is such that we would not be stretching our claims by saying that this damage is endemic in the human situation. There is not a single one of us that can claim not to have been contaminated by false views about ourselves. At this point, the Christian story in its traditional version (for there are several versions on offer, historically) has much to answer for. Since this is not designed as a theological treatise I will limit my evidence and comments to the task in hand, but we should notice in passing the contribution of the Christian church to the ongoing neuroses of millions of people. The official Christian story continues to call such damage "Original Sin" (or even "Total Depravity", in the interpretation of John Calvin). As Harvey Cox (himself a radical theologian) wrote:

> *By the nineteenth century...Kierkegaard, Marx, and Nietzsche had to become enemies of Christendom to*

> *make themselves heard. Each was condemned by the church but each was right in his own way. Kierkegaard taught that the only real sin was 'the despairing refusal to be one's self'...As Kierkegaard, Marx and Nietzsche saw, to be a man...means accepting the terrifying duty of deciding who I will be rather than merely introjecting the stereotypes that others assign to me.* [1976, p.xvf]

It may not be an exaggeration to say, therefore, that the Church, at least in its official position following Augustine and his pronouncements, has a vested interest in maintaining this low view of humankind since it is in the business of offering salvation from the sin they seek to maintain as the very nature of every human being. Some theologians and, more to the point of our present discussion, psychotherapists, have entered the lists to refute this common and prevailing view.

Carl Rogers, the founder of Client-Centred Therapy, was brought up in a Christian fundamentalist family. Brian Thorne, his biographer, writes:

> *Julia Rogers, Carl's mother, would herself often conduct family prayers and one of her favourite biblical quotations on these occasions was the scarcely encouraging verse: "All our righteousness is as filthy rags in thy sight, O Lord" (Isaiah 64: 6) The choice of text is revealing for it points to a view of human nature which regards human beings as essentially corrupt. Such a view is commonplace in many Christian circles but nowhere more so than in strict, Evangelical churches where the 'fallenness' of man is a central tenet and is accompanied by an emphasis on the judgement of God and the eternal punishment for sinners who do not turn to a personal Saviour by whose*

> *sacrificial blood alone they can be saved from damnation.* [*Carl Rogers and the Doctrine of Original Sin*, Person-Centred Review, 5, (4), 1990]

Small wonder that, with this kind of family background,

> *...together with the attacks made upon him by Christian writers steeped in the Augustinian notion of Original Sin meant that to the end of his life [Rogers] saw Christianity as essentially hostile to human nature and caught up in guilt-inducing judgementalism.* [Brian Thorne, 1992, p.81]

To be fair to the Church, there are welcome signs that many members of the Christian faith are unhappy with the Augustinian position and

> *'the more ancient spiritual tradition of original righteousness and original blessing is being rediscovered ... and with it the hopefulness for human evolution which is characteristic of Rogers' viewpoint.* [Brian Thorne, *ibid.*]

This optimistic view also lies behind the 'OK' position introduced by Eric Berne. Whereas the popular interpretation of the Christian story maintains that – by nature – we are 'Not OK', the emphasis made by the humanistic psychologies is that we are – by nature – 'OK'. This means that underneath our masks and other defensive stratagems, hiding what we consider to be all the bad and awful truths about our inner self, there is actually a deeper, Good Self which each of us needs to dis/cover. To that end, therapeutic approaches of all the major humanistic schools are directed.

HEALING THE DIVIDED SELF

In order to become my Self, I must be open to the various parts of myself, both the familiar and the unfamiliar, the acceptable and the unacceptable, the welcomed parts as well the unwelcome. Healing, therefore, is to be understood neither in terms of denial of our unacceptable parts ("That's not me!") nor by a total identification with them ("You're right' I'm all bad!"). Rather, healing is best understood in terms of integration (Latin: *integrare*: 'make whole'.)

This does not mean some kind of homogenous mass whereby my Self resembles a set of coloured plasticine strips all pressed together to make an unattractive grey lump. It means the acceptance of my different parts in the same way as orchestral sounds emanate from a variety of instruments, which the composer uses to convey his or her music. Each instrument has its own value and contribution. So whereby the instruments are playing different parts and maybe even be playing at different tempi or notes, they are integrated, controlled by, the conductor and what we hear is, say, Beethoven's Fourth Piano Concerto.

In this concerto, Beethoven sets up a kind of dialogue within the music. In the second movement, the piano begins softly and meditatively, but the strings will have none of this. They interrupt the piano's peaceful melody with a different, *fortissimo*, tonal quality, angrily cutting across and trying to drown out the piano's contribution. The piano, however, persists only to be denied its place in the musical scheme by the string section. As the movement develops, however, one becomes aware of a change taking place. The strings are less aggressive, taking on some of the quieter themes introduced by the piano, and ending with a sense of agreement and harmony.

To me, this piece resembles an argument between the masculine and feminine aspects within the psyche, a gentle woman and an aggressive man, who eventually achieve reconciliation. While both remain themselves, they appear to be more aware of one another. They both have a place in the concerto and do not have to be seen as rivals or as competitors. They can be integrated. They can co-exist.

Perhaps the healing of the psyche may be seen through this familiar and musical metaphor. While there may be 'dominant characteristics' within us, we need to remember that there are also more subtle, less obvious, aspects of the Self that go to make up the complexity of what we call human nature. Most studies in psychopathology reveal that anti-social and psychopathic tendencies emerge when only one part of the psyche governs our behaviour: "Always this; Never that!" = neurosis.

GENDER ISSUES

This phenomenon can be most easily identified when we consider gender issues, particularly as the Women's Movement of the last quarter of the twentieth-century has pushed them to the top of the social agenda.

The previously accepted definitions of what is male and what is female have come under intense scrutiny, and one of the most important factors to have emerged is the rediscovery that men and woman have become stereotyped – polarized – in such a way that distortion has occurred. It must be admitted that such polarization has been chiefly the result of a dominant masculine and patriarchal influence and partly the acquiescence and collusion of female reaction patterns. Both of these have become the focus of attention in the past forty years or so and while the discussion has often been heated, and on occasions aggressive, nevertheless the beneficial effect is being seen in the new awareness of gender issues across the whole political, personal, commercial and psychological spectra. For our present purposes, however, it is important to note the effects of a revision of attitudes upon the twenty-first century corporate consciousness.

Whereas the traditional view of woman meant that their 'masculine' traits had to be denied or concealed, it was equally true that the 'feminine' traits of men had also to be suppressed. This old polarization is gradually giving way to a more healthy integration of both feminine and masculine attributes, and in the process a re-definition of what these attributes actually consist of is a topic of debate. For example, Sam Keen writes:

> *There is an obvious difference between men and woman, but that has no relationship to the supposed differences between 'masculine' and 'feminine'. In my judgment, we would gain much clarity if we ceased using the words 'masculine' and 'feminine' except to refer to the stereotypes of the genders that have been historically predominant. Far better to remain with the real mystery of man and woman than the false mystification of the masculine and feminine. As nearly as I can tell, I, being a man, having nothing feminine about me. For me, feeling proud of being a man involves practicing the virtues of repentance, compassion, patience, carefulness, etc. My virility is inseparable from opening out, receiving, embracing.* [1991, p. 214]

Healthy-mindedness must be seen as an integration not only of the various 'parts' of the self, but must include this important aspect of gender. Becoming fully who I am, in touch with all of the many and contradictory aspects of my Self, is a lifelong commitment. It is an agenda for fulfilment, a programme for growth, and above all an exciting adventure that can make life worth living.

We have seen in the recent decades a massive shift in public opinion with Government legislation running to keep up: the question of 'equal opportunities', job vacancies now open to both sexes; the 'rights' of various minority groups such as the move towards the 'normalisation' of homosexual Civil Partnerships. Many aspects of our corporate life have been broadened out and in some cases it has involved the removal of some masks that had been formerly adopted in order to prevent shame or disgrace. British Society is becoming more 'open' but there is still much ground to make up. None of this 'progress' has happened without some resistance in some quarters, and not just by 'Disgusted of Tunbridge Wells"! The manufacturers of masks will not let their industry decline without a fight. There are many vested interests in maintaining the *status quo*.

We need to challenge head-on all those factors and family members that contributed to the writing of our personal story, those 'ghost-writers' who tried to tell us who we were. No one is under any illusion what this may cost us, but it is 'costing us' anyway by not becoming who we truly are.

We shall examine in our next chapter how we can rid ourselves of those elements in our background and education that have contributed to our false self-image, and our need for masks, in order to emerge with a greater belief in our self-esteem and personal worth and value.

CHAPTER FIVE
Theme: Decisions

WRITING OUR OWN LIFE-SCRIPT

What is this self inside us, this silent observer,
severe and speechless critic, who can terrorise us
and urge us on to futile activity,
and in the end, judge us still more severely
for the errors into which his own reproaches drove us.
(The Elder Statesman: Faber, 1958.)

These words of T. S. Eliot are quoted in Dorothy Rowe's powerful book *Depression: The Way out of Your Prison*, [1983, p.93] in the chapter entitled "Why I won't leave the prison". Her question raises the key issue for becoming who we are: given the choice of remaining depressed or finding out and becoming who we truly are, why is that so many of us choose to remain in our personal prisons, be they that of depression or within our iron masks? For on the face of it to do so would be unthinkable, unimaginable, foolish. After all, who would prefer to choose imprisonment rather than freedom? Does anyone?

The sad – and to the ordinary person in the street,

inexplicable – fact is that many people do make that unimaginable decision. Some people find making the decision to find out and become who they truly are so threatening that, according to William Shakespeare, it *"makes us bear those ills we have than fly to others that we know not of"*. Interestingly, from the point of view of the subject of this book, this quotation comes from Hamlet's 'Soliloquy' (*Hamlet*, Act 3, Scene 1, l. 89) which begins by asking, *"To be or not to be? That is the question..."*

Of course, the question itself implies that we have a choice in the matter of our personal discovery. First, I will detail several reasons why some of us prefer to choose to remain in our prison, governed by the Lion, the Witch and their accursed Wardrobe, rather than seek liberation. Secondly, I will outline some of the implications of choosing to become who we truly are. And, lastly, I will suggest some practical ways of re-writing the personal agenda others have lumbered us with and to emerge from our iron masks. In brief, how to discard our personal 'severe and speechless critic'.

1. OK: SO YOU'RE IN PRISON. BUT REMEMBER: YOU HAVE SWALLOWED THE KEY!

This is one of the basic premises of all psychotherapy and counselling: the key to the client's healing lies within himself or herself, not within the therapist. A colleague of mine I worked with in Chicago wrote this to his friends as would-be therapists:

Your freedom will threaten the self-imprisoned. Don't

> *enter their dungeons to do battle. Such prisoners swallow their own keys. They can only be retrieved in one of two ways, neither of which is pleasant. And they may swallow their keys again anyway. Better to show them how to do without keys and chains entirely. Call them out.*

So, let's not make the mistake of thinking that everyone is just longing to be set free from the conditioning of their past. But what lies behind such refusal? In other words, what is the nature of the power that our often neurotic *status quo* holds over us?

The Fear of Change

Part of the pain that many people suffer boils down to the following Litany:

- Better the devil you know…
- Yes, my life is a mess – I'm a mess – but maybe changing it is not such a good idea!
- Even if I don't like who I am, at least I'm familiar with it!
- Supposing others don't like the new me, what then?
- My loved ones have got used to my iron mask – why upset them by removing it?
- I've worn my "I'm Stupid!" T-Shirt for years: it seems to fit. I don't like getting into anything new.
- Maybe my parents were right: I probably am bad.

The fear of change lies behind all these familiar yet pathetic excuses. Sometimes this is expressed even by people who go into therapy precisely to make such life-enhancing changes. Sheldon Kopp is right when he says:

> *And so, it is not astonishing that, though the patient enters therapy insisting that he wants to change, more often than not, what he really wants is to remain the same and to get the therapist to make him feel better. He prefers the security of known misery to the misery of unfamiliar insecurity.* [1979, p.2]

Kopp puts his finger unerringly on the fundamental need for security. This is what often lies behind our fear of change. The choice that appears to be set before us is this: do I struggle on with my old Self, or do I struggle on with finding the real Self? Either way, a struggle is going to be involved. There is no easy way out of our prison.

The Fear of what others might say

Other people have probably got used to who we are, masks and all. We may not be the easiest person in the world to get on with, but at least we are predictable; other people more or less know what to expect. In close, intimate relationships, we get used to one another's foibles and 'funny ways' but at least we know what to expect. I have worked with dozens of former clients whose chief worry was what their partners would say if they chose to change any of the scripts their relationships had been founded upon. They have told me –

- Ooh! I could never say that! He'd kill me
- She'd not take that sitting down
- But, I've always done it that way
- If I did that, she'd leave
- I could never speak to my husband like that
- She doesn't like changes

This is the language and vocabulary of *fear*. I am in no way underestimating the effects that our personal change could have on the lives of our significant others. The feared responses by other people often have a salutary effect upon our choices, and frequently consist of a variation of the painful theme of rejection. Most of us have had quite enough rejection in our lives without inviting more. Maybe it's better to stay inside our prison…

The Fear of Consequences

Becoming who we truly are has inevitable consequences not only for our own lives but also for the lives of those people who matter to us. We may have to face up to a catalogue of things that can threaten us enough to make us stay behind our mask.

** our job

Among those choosing to change, it is a frequent experience to discover that they are working in the wrong job. My own personal theory is that jobs choose us, not the other way round. What I mean is this: there can be an uncanny 'fit' between how we have been constituted and jobs that seem to attract us.

Jack suffered from a crippling sense of inferiority. He was dissatisfied with life in general and his job in the factory in particular. He decided out of the blue to become an ambulance driver. After retraining, and getting used to the involvement with members of the public, he seemed a far happier person. Until, quite suddenly, he descended into a clinical depression. No one could understand this, least of all Jack himself. It was only through intensive counselling that the solution appeared. Jack's inferiority complex led him to believe in his own lack of worth, and in an anticipation of his rejection by others, as 'not good enough'. No one, he felt, was ever pleased to see him. "How did those needing an ambulance feel when you arrived?" the counsellor asked. "Oh, that was quite different," Jack said. "Everyone was just waiting for me, and welcomed me with open arms! I liked that." The counsellor asked again, "Was that welcome always given?" "Yes," said Jack, "except on that last occasion I went to work." What transpired was that an ambulance that Jack was driving was called to man who had had a heart attack, but by the time the ambulance arrived, the man had died. His depression was triggered by the vehement complaints by the man's wife that he had taken too long in coming. "I felt so rejected, " said Jack. What he only gradually came to recognise was that his so-called free choice in changing jobs was motivated by his unconscious need for acceptance. The job chose him, in order to meet those needs. "After all," thought Jack, "Everyone is pleased to see an ambulance driver!" He hadn't calculated for the unexpected. By raising his own self-esteem, Jack eventually came to realise that he could find acceptance from within himself, and enjoy his job with the Ambulance service free from hidden motivation.

** our partner and family

Many couples, wrestling with the intricacies of partnerships, live in fear of creative change. They fear not only admitting to those parts of themselves that have emerged into their consciousness (yet remain hidden from those they love), but also the rejection that they fear would almost certainly be the consequence of such disclosure.

Jane was an exceptional student. As a vicar's wife, she had never really felt comfortable with the stereotypical image of Oxfam clothing rejects and making tea for the Mothers' Union.

She had a degree in biochemistry but the parishioners expressed the hope that she would be a 'proper vicar's wife' and set a good example to the parish by not going out to work. She felt she was decaying mentally and spiritually. She decided to study for a Diploma in Counselling by distance learning from a local theological college. "The parishioners need not know about that," Jane thought. But as she progressed through the required texts for reading, she found a welcome release from the stultifying religious language she had been immersed in from childhood. She encountered Humanistic Psychology that had a very firm belief system different from the Christian model. She read widely and avidly, and found herself moving away from the strict Evangelical beliefs of her own family and also that of her husband. How could she tell him what was happening? What would become of their Christian partnership in church work? Could he cope with a manifest breach in their previous solidarity of faith? Staying within her prison may at least make Jane feel safe, but the long-term damage to her own inner integrity would be immense.

Other consequences to a marriage include taking another look at the things that we have allowed our partner to do to us within the relationship. Imbalances in the delicate structure of living with another person may come under painful scrutiny. Issues of *control* will doubtless be one such focus of attention. Dependency, also. Challenging the previously unexamined and unchallenged *status quo* is always tricky. For some people, so threatening are such potential changes that they prefer to stay behind their iron masks. They choose to stay on 'auto-pilot'.

So there are some formidable issues to face as we consider taking the steps necessary to becoming who we are. Not everyone is going to like or accept a radical change in our identity. For some, the threat is too much for them and they choose to remain in their prison of conformity. They will go on wearing the old T-shirts others have given them and by which they will continue to identify themselves. Of course, people are free to make that choice but at least they may now know that there are different choices that they can make – perhaps when they have grown stronger and do not need the approval or acceptance of others in quite the same way. Remember: they have swallowed their own key.

Others, however, have had enough of allowing other people to tell them who they are and are now ready for change. How can they do this?

2. "YOU CAN FLY – BUT THAT CHRYSALIS HAS JUST GOT TO GO!"

Entering the office of a therapist in Kansas City, I noticed an enormous banner adorning the reception area. It showed a gorgeous, multi-coloured butterfly – the image and symbol of freedom and resurrection – with these words sewn into the pattern. I have watched the primal struggle for birth when my own children were born, and – in common with most paternal reactions – the experience is truly awe-inspiring. Some births appear quite natural and with apparent ease, while others seem to be engaged in a never-ending struggle to enter the world. I remember watching the gyrations of a small, brown chrysalis one day at a Butterfly Farm. The chrysalis was swinging precariously and I was aware of the eternal struggle to be born in its new form. For those of us who take the risk of becoming who we have it in us to be, it is like watching our own struggle. Perhaps we could envisage a dialogue between the caterpillar and the butterfly: the earth-bound caterpillar laughing at the weird fantasies of ever flying, and others in attendance joining in the gales of uncontrollable laughter: "You? Fly? Don't be so daft!" Yet, as I watched the chrysalis slowly turning, slowly but surely the newborn butterfly emerged ready to dry its wings and begin a new creation. For me, it was – and always is – a miracle, a wholly numinous event.

For those of us who are therapists, there is always the privilege of seeing some of those 'caterpillars' we counsel turning into beautiful butterflies. They come crawling in on hands and knees sometimes, and after what can seem like an eternity they emerge from their cocoons of habit and conditioning and fulfil their own inner potential. Yet, there is a salutary warning to therapists found in the writings of Nikos Kazantzakis:

> *Once, I remembered I had detached a chrysalis from the trunk of an olive tree and placed it in my palm. Inside the transparent coating I discerned a living thing. It was moving. The hidden process must have reached its terminus; the future, still enslaved butterfly was waiting with silent tremors for the sacred hour when it would emerge into the sunlight. It was not in a hurry. Having the confidence in the light, the warm air, in God's eternal law, it was waiting.*
>
> *But I was in a hurry. I wanted to see the miracle hatch before me as soon as possible, wanted to see how the body surges out of the tomb and shroud to become a living soul. Bending over, I began to blow my warm breath over the chrysalis, and behold! A slit soon incised itself on the chrysalis's back, the entire shroud gradually split from top to bottom, and the immature, bright green butterfly appeared, still tightly locked together, its wings*

> *twisted, its legs glued to its abdomen. It squirmed gently and kept coming more and more to life beneath my warm, persistent breath. One wing as pale as a budding poplar leaf disengaged itself from the body and began to palpitate, struggling to unfold along its entire length, but in vain. It stayed half opened, shrivelled. Soon the other wing moved as well, toiled in its own right to stretch, was unable to, and remained half unfolded and trembling. I, with a human being's effrontery, continued to lean over and blow my warm exhalation upon the maimed wings, but they had ceased to move now and had drooped down, as still and lifeless as a stone.*
>
> *I felt sick at heart. Because of my hurry, because I had dared to transgress an eternal law. I had killed the butterfly. In my hand I held a carcass. Years and years have passed, but that butterfly's weightless carcass has weighed heavily on my conscience ever since.* [1973, p. 465f.]

These words, I believe, should be inscribed upon every therapist's charter. They warn of impatience, the 'effrontery' of trying to speed up a process that has its own momentum and timescale. Acting as a psychological midwife involves waiting for the ripe moment for the newly born to emerge. If we continue our analogy, there is always a necessary process of gestation until that right moment is reached: to hurry it can end in death, as poor Kazantzakis discovered. The Greek language itself in which, of course, Kazantzakis wrote, has two quite different words for 'time'. One is chronos (Χρονος - as in chronology), which is measured time – the time on our watches. The other word is kairos (Καιρος – the ripe moment) that determines when the farmer goes in to harvest his wheat.

Being born is more a matter of kairos rather than chronos. Many times I have been asked by clients, "How long will this take?" "When the kairos is right," is the only truthful answer that can be given. (We shall examine this distinction further in our next chapter.)

This salutary tale of Kazantzakis, therefore, has a wider relevance than just the practice of psychotherapy. It applies to all of us who decide to engage in the struggle to be born into who we truly are. What will this involve and how do we go about it?

3. THE LION, THE WITCH AND THE WARDROBE REVISITED.

In Chapter Two, we noticed how this familiar title from C. S. Lewis's Narnia tales might usefully describe how our original distortion of identity came about. The Lion represented power: the power that parents and others exercise and that appears to the newborn infant as absolute. The Witch represented the malign influences over us, often in a Fairy Godmother disguise. If the Lion represented an abuse of power, and the Witch an abuse of trust, then the subsequent Wardrobe they supplied us with represented an abuse of our individuality.

The struggle to become who we are involves taking a fresh look at such influences. Paradoxically, in order to progress we must regress. We need to name and identify these past influences over us at our impressionable stages of development. This is usually possible by looking into our personal wardrobes to see what we find there and who gave us our outfits by which we have come to identify ourselves. What are the logos on some of our inherited T-shirts?

Again and again in counselling it is found that when people begin to tell others who they are, and how they feel about being who they are, the person they think they are is not the person that others recognise at all.

"Zena" swept into my counselling room looking like a million dollars. The make-up was subtle but used to good effect. She had long legs and a good bearing and appeared full of self-confidence. I began to wonder why she had made the appointment to see me. She was quite stunning. Yet, she spent her first hour pouring out a story of self-doubt, self-rejection and total inferiority. The person she told me she felt herself to be in no way coincided with the person I was beholding. She pulled herself down like this: "My nose is too long, my breasts too small!" She wept as she told me how ugly she felt, and wondered if she should find the money for a breast-implant. Each relationship that broke up was accounted for by her feelings of unattractiveness. This in turn resulted in morbid jealousy. She would not allow her male partners to watch Miss World – that was a red rag to the proverbial bull. "Breast-seller"-type books were also banned and television viewing was severely censored. Needless to say, her partners found such behaviour totally unacceptable, and nothing they could say to affirm her attractiveness and desirability made any difference. In desperation, she sought therapy.

She told me, quite seriously, that she was the Ugly Duckling of the family. Her sisters were all far better looking than Zena. Now it does not take several degrees in psychology and training as a therapist to notice the discrepancy in the story. It was clear to the most drunken fly on the wall that she was most certainly not an Ugly Duckling. But, the discipline of counselling involves us in taking the story at face value and to honour her feelings and not to contradict them as everyone else around was doing. My inevitable question to such people as Zena is this: "Who told you that you were an Ugly Duckling?"

Gradually the story unfolded. She was a victim of a Pride of Lions and Witches, and she had ended up with a wardrobe of T-shirts that displayed, "I am the Ugly Duckling!" I gently reminded her that she was not born with that knowledge. How did she come by those T-shirts? Who inscribed that Logo on the front? How long had she been wearing them (feeling like this)?

At once she recognised their origins. The chrysalis began to stretch and then burst, and eventually over a period of time she could accept her own goodness and own the technicoloured wings that nature had blessed her with. She could undress in front of a mirror now and feel good about her body. She had to hand those T-shirts back to those in her past who had put them on her and told her who she was. That was now her decision. She had taken back her own power from the Lions; she began to trust herself and her own integrity that the Witches had robbed her of; and she could now discard the outworn T-shirts and choose her own set according to her new awareness of her self-image. She eventually left, wearing an "I'm OK" T-shirt and I had a sense that no longer need she fear other women nor seek to dominate men. She left her obsessive need to compare herself with other women behind her; she abandoned her controlling behaviour of her male partners. She had let the chrysalis go and now she could fly.

This was not done without an enormous amount of rage which she expressed towards the family Lions and Witches. She had accepted as a child the identity that others had imposed upon her. She had never questioned it, nor would she ever have dared do so. Lions and Witches are not easy to contradict when you are a vulnerable little child! Contradiction might mean even harsher treatment; better to go with the flow, wear the T-shirt and eventually get so used to wearing it that you forget where it came from. Worn long enough, the mask becomes part of our face, as Sheldon Kopp reminded us earlier.

Change involves mentally and emotionally handing back the wardrobe which others clothed us in. We do this by a conscious refusal to allow other people to define us and tell us who we are. Behind the negative logos others have dumped on us we begin to catch a glimpse of an original goodness, a good Self that others either did not recognise or which threatened others in some way. It is only when we discover our original goodness that we can begin to discard the outworn T-shirts and their detrimental effects they have had upon our personal identity for most of our lives. Zena might have said, "I'm not an Ugly Duckling, nor ever was, and I'm furious at you for deceiving me into believing that I was! Take this wardrobe back – it belongs to you, not me!"

Who were the Lions and the Witches of your early childhood? Maybe you were blessed with fairy godmothers that were genuinely committed to your well-being. Perhaps your world of childhood is simply packed with happy memories that helped you towards a good sense of your own Self. Sometimes it only takes one Lion to demolish that sense of goodness, as many people I have worked with will testify. That single memory can be quite sufficient to affect us for the rest of our lives. Early life seems to such people as merely survival. There is no joy, no spontaneity, no self-celebration. A Lion or a Witch destroyed all that.

Some of the Logos I have heard represent the merest tip of a social iceberg:

T-Shirt Logo	The Primal Origin
I am evil	"You wicked child!"
I am stupid	"Why are you so thick?"
I am ugly	"Get out of my sight!"
I am a waste of space	"Why don't you just leave?"
I ruined my mother's sex life	"You made me go off sex!"
I drove my father away	"Now look what you've done!"
I made my brother commit suicide	"It was all your fault!"
I brought shame on my family	"Fancy getting pregnant!"
I mess things up	"You just can't be trusted!"
I am such a whimp	"You know you can't manage!"
I can't cope	"Your brother is so skilled!"
I am not wanted	"You were a mistake!"
I am bad	"You bad boy!"
I am smelly	"You disgust me!"
I am a nuisance	"We can do without you!"
I am hungry	"You're never satisfied!"
I am too demanding	"Not now!"
I do not matter	"Can't it wait?"

Such a list is by no means exhaustive. But it is sufficient for our present purpose to notice how these primal inputs gradually erode any sense of goodness in a child, and replace this with negative identities. Again, we ask, "Who told you that?" Our Logos, therefore, are placed upon us; we actually chose none of them! And because we become so familiar with them, we gradually come to believe that we were born with them; they attain a kind of divine authority, unchallengeable and immutable. When we come to recognise that we now have a choice whether to go on wearing these Logos or not, we reach a moment of decision. There is, after all, a price to pay for knowledge. We cannot now go on believing that they are true; we must make a decision:

> *I may not be responsible for their origin, but I am now responsible if I choose to go on wearing them.*

Whichever way we decide, we must take responsibility for the scripts we live by. Emptying the wardrobe can be an exciting yet risky venture for some people. Of some unfashionable clothes we can hear ourselves saying, "That's not me any more!" and we throw them away or convey them to the Charity shop. But we must wear something. New clothes must replace the old wardrobe which represented our now outdated identities. We will not settle for a vacuum.

We say to the world, "This is the real me!" Thus it is that we move from decision to declaration – allowing the world to see our technicoloured wings and our resplendent array of new, appropriate clothing.

John Rowan, however, adds an important 'health warning' as we seek to become and declare who we really are:

> *When we get to the real self in therapy it feels awfully dangerous to go any further. This is for two different reasons: first, the way in lies through all our most negative self-images, which have been experienced as painful and shocking, and so we are scared of meeting even more, even dirtier secrets as we dig down further; and second, there seems to be something 'ultimate' about the real self, so that when we get to it, it seems like a breakthrough into a whole different world. We are promised that this different world will be better, but it is the difference which appals us. It seems that we almost have to die to get there.* [1983, p.63]

The ideas connected with 'dying' and 'resurrection' are a common feature of many religious groups, not just the Christian one. I recall one preacher saying that it was no use putting an income tax demand in the hands of a corpse! A cadaver is 'dead' to such claims. But something similar happens when we decide to change our lives, to change the basis we have been built on, to throw off the chains of infantile conditioning, and risk coming out of our prison of conformity to the wishes of other people. Like Sam's story above, [p.50] desperation is all it took to grab his father by the scruff of his neck and change the script of a lifetime.

Fritz Perls suggested a creedal formula that underlies his theory of Gestalt Therapy:

I am not in this world to live up to your expectations
and you are not in this world to live up to mine.
You are you, and I am I,
and if by chance, we find each other, it's beautiful.
If not, it can't be helped.

To some people, this creed has smacked of self-centredness and based purely on selfishness. But when we consider to what extent they are *true*, that is that many of us have believed that we exist in this world to live up to the expectations of other people, these criticisms just simply have to be faced and rejected. As Fritz Perls has reminded us: *to suffer one's death and to be reborn is not easy.*

I met "Shirley" while working as a Chaplain to a Psychiatric Hospital. She had been sectioned due to a clinical depression that had led her to make several attempts at suicide. Her life seemed meaningless, as she began to share with me how her life had been one long, unending servitude to the expectations and needs of other people. I asked her if the word "No" was within her vocabulary, and she smiled and said, "No!" We laughed at this contradiction.

I then asked her how her fortnightly consultation with her Psychiatrist was going, and she said that she found it unsatisfactory. It turned out that she would be invited into the consulting room, but there was hardly ever any eye contact between them. The doctor would ask how she felt, and she would reply, "Fine". The drugs were then renewed for another two weeks. I asked Shirley if this treatment was satisfactory to her, and she said no. She was, in fact, quite angry with her doctor for this perfunctory treatment and she often left feeling not only a nuisance but also simply dismissed. When anger surfaces, healing is never far away.

I then enquired what she would like to say to the doctor, and she was very clear that there were many aspects of her condition and treatment that she wanted to discuss. "But I daren't," she said. (The doctor was clearly fulfilling a Lion role in her economy.) We sat down and talked about she could change her behaviour, and she eventually compiled a list of things she wanted to say at her next appointment. I accompanied her to the office, and gave her an encouraging smile as she disappeared through the door.

"Good afternoon. Everything still going well?" asked the doctor, consulting his notes.

Taking a deep breath, she managed to stammer, "No! Things are not going well."

The doctor's face shot up from his file and he looked at her for the first time she could remember. Shirley trembled, and she sat down and worked her way through her list. Meanwhile, I was outside in the waiting room, counting the minutes, hoping she would find the courage to say what she wanted to say. Two minutes elapsed, then five, and then ten. Still she remained in the office. After twenty minutes she emerged, beaming from ear to ear and fell into my arms, relief all over her face. "I did it! I did it!" she exclaimed excitedly.

She found from within even her depleted resources the courage to challenge the treatment she had allowed for so long. She finally decided she would take responsibility for what she was allowing the doctor to do to her. This was merely one example of how most of her life had been lived, always dedicated to the expectations and needs of others, never putting her own into the frame. As we walked together in the grounds, I had the distinct impression that Shirley had turned a corner, had taken responsibility. I shared with her the words of Fritz Perls and she immediately saw the value of them – she was not in this world to live up to the expectations of other people, nor were they in this world to live up to hers.

Within a month, Shirley had been discharged. She began to re-orientate her life at home with her husband and children, and the last I heard from her was a letter thanking me for the role I played. She had joined her local church and was finding support and care for herself in this important transitional period.

My role had been that of an enabler: I encouraged her to find the ability within herself to turn acquiescence into creative confrontation. She had confronted the Lion in his den, and had survived.

She had broken free.

CHAPTER SIX
Theme: Deliverance

BREAKING FREE

Freedom is born in the moment
I decide I am free to move away
from what has previously imprisoned me.
[Sam Keen: 1994, p. 63]

The experiences of 'Shirley' and the others mentioned earlier epitomise Sam Keen's declaration. They *chose* to come out of their prison. The areas I shall focus upon in this chapter will be:

- the issues surrounding "life on the outside", and how we go about re-drawing a new life-map more congruent to, and expressive of, the recovery of our true Self;
- the integration of our new-found insights into a coherent pattern of daily living;
- identifying those forces that will undoubtedly be ranged against us and what weapons we can use to maintain our integrity.

It was understandable, and even necessary, that others should supply us with our first infant life-maps, however distorted we may later have discovered them to be. It is now time to grasp the nettle and set about the important task of drawing a new Life-map, one that *we* have decided upon and which declares to the world who we are. We are now in charge of deciding where we are going. Becoming the cartographer of our own psyche helps us to delineate our own boundaries.

- We claim the right to define our own destiny and to decide who we are: the word for this is *autonomy.*
- But there is a traditional enemy of autonomy: the word for this is *authority.*

THE GARDEN OF EDEN: A MYTH FOR ALL SEASONS

The battle between these two powerful forces - authority *versus* autonomy, the urge to conform and the urge to rebel - lies at the heart of all human experience, and finds meaningful expression in the familiar Biblical story. It is the "Story of Everyman and Everywoman", and it all began in the mythic Garden of Eden. The traditional interpretation of this story emphasises the goodness of God in the provision of idyllic surroundings for Adam and Eve, their disobedience in being led astray by the Serpent, and their subsequent expulsion from the Garden. But when we take a closer look at the dynamics of this myth a further truth emerges:

> *Read the myth carefully, and you will see that the Lord God, or his authorised earthly representatives, presents us with a double bind, a Hobson's choice, a lose-lose dilemma. Either: Be obedient to authority, remain in the*

> *Garden of childlike innocence, and receive the gift of happiness and immortality. Or: Exercise your freedom, gain bitter-sweet self-knowledge, judge good and evil for yourself, be expelled from the garden, earn a living by the sweat of your brow, and live with the awareness that you will die.*
>
> *The story of the Garden endures because it captures something perennial about the human condition...In due time, some crisis presents us with the challenge to develop autonomy...If we experiment and break the taboos, we may be punished and we will certainly feel guilt and be cast out of the Garden. But if we do not, if we remain obedient children, we will feel the shame that comes from never exercising our freedom and from living our own lives within the Garden of the Authorities. If we disobey, we will have to wrestle with guilt and autonomy; if we obey, we will have to wrestle with shame and dependency.* [1994, p.38f]

These words of Sam Keen portray precisely the issue at the heart of 'breaking free'. Do we 'lose' by exercising our autonomy, breaking the rules of The Authorities (God = Parents?) and experiencing shame and rejection? Or, do we 'lose' by sacrificing our autonomy and experiencing shame and dependency? It is a dilemma facing every person, and especially during the developmental period called "adolescence". In a 'no-win' situation the best advice I was ever given was to 'chose which way to lose'. In the Eden myth, Adam chose *autonomy* – and wrestled with the shame and rejection. And the mistake Adam and Eve made was in letting a snake tell them what to do. *"For us"*, says Harvey Cox [1976, p. xvii] *"it means allowing others to dictate the identities with which we live out our lives."*

The issues in this 'Authority v. Autonomy' struggle form an important 'staging post' as we journey through life. We may look back and notice to what extent other people's thinking has affected our own (the snakes), and this will be especially true as we set about our present task of breaking free. Not only do others supply us with our earliest life-maps but they also leave behind them severe warnings about tampering with them. "Here be dragons!" Warning voices will be heard whenever the thought of changing our life-map occurs, and so it is necessary to identify them in advance, otherwise they will dog us throughout our journey beyond Eden and in our map-making procedure.

SIREN VOICES

The original Sirens are found in the story of Odysseus written by Homer, the greatest poet of ancient Greece. On his journey back to Ithaca after the Trojan Wars, Odysseus sailed past the Sirens' Isle about which the goddess Circe had warned him. "Beware of their song and give their flowery meadow a wide berth."

As he approached their Island, Odysseus plugged the ears of his crew with wax, and asked them to bind him fast to the mast in case he succumbed to their alluring voice. Eventually, he heard them:

> *"Draw near," they sang, "illustrious Odysseus, flower of Achaean chivalry, and bring your ship to rest so that you may hear our voices. No seaman ever sailed his black ship past this spot without listening to the sweet tones that flow from our lips, and none that listened has not*

> *been delighted and gone on a wiser man".* [E. V. Rieu translation, 1980, p.149]

Thus entered our vocabulary the symbol of the 'Siren Voices' that seek to allure and tempt travellers away from their chosen path. We, too, will hear such voices as we begin to map out our future journey free from the influences of our past. William Bridges comments upon some of the other distractions we can expect to meet:

> *Throughout Odysseus's long journey home, he is confronted by one distraction after another…There is the song of the Sirens, which symbolised the self-destruction lurking beneath the beguiling surface of all that calls upon us to turn aside. There is the lotus fruit, which stands for all that makes us forget the journey itself and our real destination. There is Calypso's promise: 'Stay with me and you need never grow old.' That fantasy – that we can stop the on-going process of life transitions – represents the most tempting and illusory promise of all. In spite of lapses, Odysseus somehow struggled past each blandishment as he struggled through the batterings.* [1980, p.51.]

Such voices can sometimes represent to us sweet reasonableness. They can sound quite logical and even friendly, but the final question is, *Cui bono?* (Who benefits?) The Sirens appeared to be offering Odysseus something for his own good, but it was their own malignant self-interest that motivated their seduction.

You also are surrounded by those who would *appear* to have your well-being at heart, but they need careful examination. Remember: there are many people around you at the moment that have a very strong vested interest in your remaining the same as you are. Your growth might somehow threaten them, upset the *status quo*, and make them feel less secure. Some of these people – spouses, children, friends – may have a strong sense of dependency, which they expect you to fulfil on their behalf. Undoubtedly, there will be tears before bedtime.

The final charge that will be made to you, when all else has failed, is this: "How can you be so selfish?" That charge needs an answer.

SELFISHNESS? OR MY DUTY TO MYSELF?

In 1879, Henrik Ibsen finished his play, *A Doll's House*, and it was performed at the Theatre Royal in Copenhagen three weeks after its publication. It caused a major scandal, and the reasons are not hard to find. Bearing in mind the prevailing attitudes at that time regarding 'the sanctity of marriage' – a thinly veiled euphemism for traditional male domination and the enslavement of women trapped within it – the play was sensational.

In the grand climax to the play, Torvald's wife, Nora, declares that she is leaving her husband and their children. First of all, Torvald tries the well-worn ploy of accusing his wife of insanity (*"You're out of your mind...this is madness."*) But when that fails, he tries bullying her – *"I forbid it!"* Nora calmly answers Torvald's accusations:

Torvald: *But to leave your home – your husband and your children...You haven't thought of what people will say.*

Norah: *I can't consider that. All I know is that this is necessary for me.*
Torvald: *But this is disgraceful. Is this the way you neglect your most sacred duties?*
Norah: *What do you consider is my most sacred duty?*
Torvald: *Do I have to tell you that? Isn't it your duty to your husband and children?*
Norah: *I have another duty, just as sacred.*
Torvald: *You can't have. What duty do you mean?*
Norah: *My duty to myself.* [1965, p.227f]

Notice the progression of Torvald's manipulative responses to Norah's decision to leave him. When accusations of madness and his vain attempt to forbid Nora leaving do not work, he resorts to the weapon of "What will the neighbours say?" When this fails to influence Norah, he tries to induce *guilt* ("This is disgraceful!") Then he puts pressure on Norah by appealing to her conscience, her *moral* obligations, and it is precisely there that he comes unstuck: a protest too far! Norah reminds him of her sacred duty towards herself. Significantly, when this play was first performed in Germany,

> *...the theme was so unpalatable that when the play was performed in March 1880 Ibsen was forced to write a different ending. He described it as 'an act of barbarous violence against the play', but he preferred to write it himself rather than let anyone else lay hands on his work. In it, Helmer (Torvald) forces Norah to look at her sleeping children; she finds herself unable to leave them, drops her travelling bag, and sinks to the ground as the curtain falls with masculine supremacy restored and Woman relegated to her proper sphere of 'Kirche, Küche,*

> *Kinder.'* [Peter Watts, *Introduction, op.cit.* p. 18]

Ibsen's theme has been taken up in subsequent dramatic literature. The modern version for me is *Shirley Valentine.* Willy Russell memorably captures the dilemma his heroine finds herself in and how she finally fulfils her duty to herself. Like Norah in *A Doll's House*, Shirley hears the Siren voices to turn back and abandon the journey towards self-fulfilment. Finally, at the airport check-in desk, Shirley decides to remain behind on her Greek Island. Like Torvald, Joe (Shirley's husband) tries to get Shirley to change her mind. She remembers –

> *The first time he phoned me...he screamed at me. He said I must have finally gone mad. He said I was a disgrace – to the kids, to him, to meself* [shades of Torvald here]. *It was the easiest thing in the world to put the phone down on him. The second time he phoned he said you can't run away from life. I said I agreed with him an' now I'd found some life I had no intention of runnin' away from it. He started to scream an' shout again then; he said he knew all about me 'holiday romance', and how I'd made a fool of meself but, but if I stopped all this arsin' round, if I got meself home, where I belonged, he said, he said he'd promise never to mention it. I said, "The only holiday romance I've had, is with meself Joe. An'..an' I think...I've come to like meself, really.*

This is too much for Joe. He makes a fairly predictable attempt to explain Shirley's conduct: *"It's the bleeding change of life, isn't it?"* To which Shirley replies:

> *"That's right, Joe," I said, "That's right, it's a change of*

> *life. An' that's why you're wastin' your money phonin' me to try an' get me back. I'm not comin' back."*

The play ends with Shirley rehearsing what she will say to Joe when he finally arrives on the Island.

> *"Hello, I used to be the mother, I used to be your wife. But now, I'm Shirley Valentine again. Would you like to join me in a drink?"* [1989, p.35f.]

As was *A Doll's House* for the late Victorians, so *Shirley Valentine* is a story for our own times – a woman daring to extricate herself from the mindless round of cooking and shopping and, in Shirley's case, of talking to the kitchen wall. Whenever you finally choose to go sane – to break free – notice how many people around you accuse you of going mad!

But we do have to face such accusations, including that of being totally self-centred, if only to satisfy ourselves. Traditionally, this is enough to bring the best of us to heel, but instead, let us find a more positive answer to these charges.

In the patterns of our early childhood, morality seemed to centre on 'not being selfish'. Beneath this threat of 'being selfish' many nasty things appear to lurk. To be selfish is apparently the unforgivable sin. To pay attention to our own self and its needs is traditionally taught as a Very Bad Thing Indeed. Others must always come first. In other words, our very first lessons in the School of Life teach us that our needs don't matter, it is only other people who have needs, and it is our duty to put others before ourselves. Self-sacrifice is elevated to the Supreme Virtue.

Small wonder that, like Adam and Eve, we must go through paroxysms of guilt and shame in order to fulfil our own potential. One client said to me it was like challenging the Ten Commandments. Why do characters like Norah and Shirley Valentine have to run the gauntlet of accusations of selfishness and the abandonment of their supreme duty? Because people like Torvald and Joe sense that *their power base is under threat*, and life will be too uncomfortable for them without their patient and conforming wives to smooth their matrimonial path. Dr. Julian Hafner elaborates on a further interesting fact that may tie in subconsciously with objections to change:

> *Several studies have found that young men and women experience very similar levels of anxiety and depression. Women show no increase in psychiatric disorder as they get older – unless they get married. Single women over the age of thirty-five report no more anxiety and depression than single women in their twenties. But the situation is quite different for single men, who experience more psychiatric disorder as they get older. The picture that emerges from most studies is clear: overall, the mental health of women deteriorates after marriage. But for men, marriage has the opposite effect, enhancing their mental health, or at least protecting them from the psychological deterioration shown by their unmarried fellows.* [1993, p.7]

Whenever others try to divert us from our journey into wholeness and self-discovery, it is they who are portraying true selfishness. They do not wish us well on the journey of self-celebration; they condemn us. They do not see the benefits accruing to us by such a decision; no, they see only their own personal inconvenience. They see nothing of their own part in our previous self-destruction; they are aware only of the alarming prospect of the loss of their creature comforts and the unacceptable nuisance of having to find a replacement. Like the Sirens, like Torvald and Joe, they do their best to deflect us from our chosen path. They use any dirty tricks that come to hand: allurements, the inducement of guilt and shame, bargaining and vague promises, and finally the charge of being either insane or self-centred. Very well, then. Let us take these charges seriously for a moment.

UNSELFISHNESS: VIRTUE OR VICE?

Because the prevailing wisdom propagates a doctrine of unselfishness, as if it belonged to the moral fabric of the universe, very few of us have ever challenged this concept. It just sounds right, doesn't it? Isn't it what we are supposed to aspire to? Don't we admire this in other people and reward them by setting them up as examples for the rest of us to follow? But…take a closer look.

Erich Fromm offers us a refreshingly honest assessment of such ideas:

> *The 'unselfish' person 'does not want anything for himself'; he 'lives only for others', is proud that he does not consider himself important. He is puzzled to find that in spite of his unselfishness he is unhappy, and that his relationships to those closest to him are unsatisfactory. Analytic work shows that his unselfishness is not something apart from his other symptoms but one of them, in fact often the most important one; that he is paralysed in his capacity to love or to enjoy anything; that he is pervaded by hostility towards life and that*

> *behind the façade of unselfishness a subtle but no less intense self-centredness is hidden.* [1975, p.55]

This salvo is nothing less than a full-frontal assault on our old inherited scripts, maintaining – I believe with good reasons – that there can be as much neurosis in the 'unselfish' person as in the 'selfish' one. Those of us who see clients in psychotherapy often witness the suicidal unhappiness of those with a Martyr Complex, so far does their allegiance to the Unselfish Quest drive them. Some aspects of the Christian church have done nothing to set forward an alternative to such a quest – rather, it has added a religio-social dimension in the war against 'unselfishness'. It is not only our parents that require us to put others first: God Himself now imposes this duty upon us! At times there is a humorous dimension to this race to be Humbler Than Thou. What, however, is not funny at all are the dreadful effects they have on their own lives as well as those of their families.

Here I must make a personal confession: I have to admit to being a former paid-up member of the Denial-of-Self Society. I excelled at it; after all, as a priest was not this part of my calling, to lead from the front, giving the flock an example to follow? How proud I felt when, assisting in the 1971 census in my parish, I discovered that only one person on my list worked more hours per week than I did! My zeal for self-sacrifice knew no bounds. This was unselfishness *par excellence*. My diary knew no boundaries either, consisting of an elastic quality. Days off were a luxury since no parochial call upon my time could be denied. "Spare time" had to be spent in sermon preparation, or preparing for the regular committee meetings. Even cutting the vicarage grass was a guilt-laden experience since the parishioners would wonder why I wasn't out paying visits. In spite of my wife sending round to the vestry a message that she was leaving home, little in fact ever changed. Since the Vicar I worked under was also a workaholic, we colluded together in ignoring days off and played a kind of "Open All Hours" policy in running the parish.

The truth, I was later to discover much to my chagrin, was that we were allowing the parish to run us! But how good that made us feel? We were being Unselfish – and failed to notice the disintegrating family life around us. God knows the damage I did to my own family in following what was expected of me. It was one thing to deny myself; it was quite another to deny my family – but then, weren't we showing the rest of the parish how unselfish families ought to behave? Ready and willing to serve others first? Putting our own needs last? This, after all, was what God required of us. *"If any man would come after me, let him deny himself and take up his cross and follow me."* (Matthew 16. 24) Unselfishness, therefore, was part of the Gospel I espoused.

What pangs of guilt I endured when, finally coming to my senses, I began to demarcate 'days off' from parish work. It felt like utter failure and I recall the conflict between my duty to my parish and the duty to my family. I cannot recall when my 'conversion' eventually took place, but I do remember one salient thought from a friend of mine. I confessed to the struggle involved in denying oneself against other biblical injunctions to 'love thy neighbour *as thyself*. The reply is etched on my brain: "Tony, have you ever thought that Jesus was asking you to deny only your self-denying Self?" It took years of therapy and growth before I finally emerged from the struggle, and understood what my friend had meant. In that process, I realised with a sense of horror just how much I had despised myself. I uncovered a quite primal negative script about my own being, reinforced by an inferiority complex the size of a bus. I found that my 'unselfishness' was in fact a disguised form of compulsive selfishness, adopted as a vain attempt to give my failing ego at least some semblance of acceptance and self-esteem. I found that I had never accepted myself. It was not a struggle to 'deny myself'; that came naturally to me. Hanging it round some isolated Gospel texts merely reinforced it, and gave it a kind of divine approval. The denial of my family was often a cop-out; did I have to be *that* busy? No. It just kept my conscience quiet. 'The parish' could cover a multitude of sins, and after all, it was how I earned my living.

I recall one experience in therapy, one of many that was life changing for me. It was the day I learned how to cry. It had never occurred to me that adults could cry – weren't tears just for children, or women? The pain in my gut was so intense that great sobs came up from deep within me. My stomach ached, my chest seemed to be breaking up, and my throat did not seem to want my primal scream to emerge. (Persistent tonsillitis throughout my life, of course, was now understood in a new light.) Finally the tears came – hot, salty water pouring down my face. Every muscle in my face began to ache and I remember thinking that a grotesque mask was being ripped away from my face. It was so painful that I thought my face was coming away with the mask and that there would be no face left at the end of it. Years of conditioning rolled away: being Mr. Nice Guy, Mr. Happy Vicar, had reinforced the mask and had congealed with my real face for most of my life. Underneath, I found a new face, more real, more vulnerable, but mine. And this face was good. Eventually I began to find a self-acceptance I had never known before. In spite of this, however, the time and, more importantly, the money spent on therapy, were resented by my family.

My previous addiction to 'unselfishness' was, underneath, a vain attempt to clutch at some kind of survival without having to take the lid off my psyche. The process of doing this, however, was labelled 'selfish' – and I suppose there is a certain irony in this: perhaps we do have to risk being thought of as selfish in order to find our Self. So, unselfish behaviour, as Erich Fromm discovered years ago, can be a cloak, a barrier against total honesty and integrity. By putting my deepest needs in the centre of my concern I attracted the charge of being self-centred. Linguistically, I think this is desirable, but since 'self-centred' has a long history of being regarded as something totally discreditable and offensive, perhaps we have to change this round to 'Centred in my Self'. Finding our centre is a crying need for all of us.

SELF-LOVE: IS IT REALLY NARCISSISM?

I return to Erich Fromm for the sanest and clearest explanation of the difference between self-love and narcissism, for even Freud mistook them for the same phenomenon:

> *It is assumed that to the degree to which I love myself I do not love others, that self-love is the same as selfishness. This view goes far back in Western thought...Freud speaks of self-love [as] the same as narcissism, the turning of the libido towards oneself. Freud assumed that love is the manifestation of libido, and that the libido is either turned towards others – love; or towards oneself – self-love. Love and self-love are thus mutually exclusive in the sense that the more there is of one, the less there is of the other. If self-love is bad, if follows that unselfishness is virtuous.* [1975, p.52]

It is in the face of such confusion that many would-be pilgrims give up their journey into wholeness and finding their true Self. Their choice is between varying degrees of unhappiness: do I remain unhappy for fulfilling my potential, or unhappy because I do not? - the oldest choice going back to the Garden of Eden. But consider Fromm's explanation of a way out of this confusion:

> *The idea expressed in the Biblical 'Love thy neighbour as thyself" implies that respect for one's own self, cannot be separated from respect and love and understanding for another individual. The love for my own self is inseparably connected with the love for any other being... love of others and love of ourselves are not alternatives. From this it follows that my own self must be as much an object of my love as another person.* [*ibid.*]

So self-love is not to be confused with narcissism, the excessive concern for our false self and its defences, as Alexander Lowen rightly implies in the title of his useful book: *Narcissism: Denial of the True Self* [1985]. Rather than narcissism being an affirmation of our true self, it is actually a further denial of it. The true narcissist actually hates himself and substitutes his true self for an image of how he would like to be. It was, after all, with his *image* that the original Narcissus fell in love, not his Self.

Fromm explains this strange behaviour:

> *Selfishness and self-love, far from being identical, are actually opposites. The selfish person does not love himself too much but too little; in fact he hates himself. This lack*

> *of fondness and care for himself, which is only one expression of his lack of productiveness, leaves him empty and frustrated. He is necessarily unhappy and anxiously concerned to snatch from life the satisfactions which he blocks himself from attaining.* [1975, p.54]

It appears, therefore, that Ibsen's Norah and her sacred duty to herself was years in front of modern psychological research. Indeed, it could be seen as a recovery of the original intention of the Gospel command to love our neighbour as our Self.

THE DECLARATION OF MY TRUE SELF

It is one thing to begin to learn how to truly love oneself; it is quite another to explain this to our significant others. Is it not something best kept to ourselves in order to avoid embarrassing others? In spite of the apparent reasonableness of such an idea, it would in fact be a further denial of our selves, and that is something we have been trying to correct.

One way of viewing the idea of self-declaration is to examine again those early T-Shirt Logos and begin to replace them. (Turn back to p.115 to recall what some of them said.) Here is a tentative list of new logos more congruent with someone who has learned to feel good about themselves, to be centred in their own sense of goodness and to exhibit their sense of self-worth. They may sound brash, bragging even, but perhaps that is how they are bound to appear to order for us to correct the negativity of our past.

I have intelligence
I love my body

It feels good to be me
I'm OK
My needs are important
I am loved
I am growing

Louis Proto suggests that these are *'confidence-building affirmations'* [1990, p.143] that represent the authentic voice of that inner core that John Rowan explained (see p.89), our True Self. They may sound strange but that is because we may never have contemplated life without our defences, life outside our iron masks, life outside the False Self.

Most of us have never heard these inner voices before. They were stifled, in some cases, even before we were born, and most certainly during our childhood. Once we left our primal sense of goodness behind and entered into our negative and defended self-image, we had forgotten those voices. They simply faded away. But once we abandon the negative self-image and rediscover the good self that we truly are, such affirmations seem perfectly normal, even necessary.

Such is the social and family conditioning that other people come to expect that we will, as a matter of course, put ourselves down. If we *are* praised, we are expected to dismiss such affirmation or at least decency may require us to make several discounts. Think how many times you have been told it is wrong to 'blow your own trumpet', that we mustn't 'give him a big head', that pride is one of the 'Seven deadly sins'. These are the significant barriers to declaring ourselves to be OK – we run the risk of being thought 'big-headed'. In all my considerable experience of counselling, I have never ever come across any client complaining of a 'big head'. On the contrary, I have counselled hundreds who come in feeling beaten down, and whose self-esteem is just about at carpet level. We do not give children 'big heads' when we praise them for being who they are and for what they have done. Encouragement works better than criticism in producing well-rounded adults.

COMPONENTS OF OUR NEW LIFE MAP

I am often fascinated when, browsing around dusty second-hand bookshops, I find old maps of the early cartographers. Some of those first attempts look almost comical, but then I recall that they had only the most basic instruments with which to measure coastlines and contours. The wonder is that, when the first satellite photographs of the British Isles appeared, so many of those early maps were almost spot-on. How wrong they were – but then, how right? In those far-off days, anything was better than nothing. There is a similarity, I believe, for those of us who wish to make a more accurate and reliable map of the Self.

The psyche, of course, is not amenable to photography. To a certain extent, continents and islands are more or less stable; even though there may be slow erosion of some coastlines, their overall shape and contours remain largely the same. The psyche, however, is a dynamic not static phenomenon; it is invisible, hidden even from its 'owner'. Yet, we have discovered that what we call the 'map' of our psyche has been mainly drawn up by others who have had influence over us, who have defined us, described us, and given us our identity. Upon conscription into the Royal Air Force, I was given a new identity: I was no longer Tony, but 2452596, Air Craftsman Second Class Gough, A. W. My civilian clothes were sent home and I was given a new uniform. My hair was shaved off and I became part of group. All my individuality was removed. Autonomy disappeared and Authority reigned supreme.

Re-drawing a new map will take account of our personal history but cease to allow history to determine our future. Our own re-drawn map allows us to put the record straight.

As we noticed above, there are plenty of people (with vested interests of their own to retain the *status quo*) who will try to deflect us from our project. The 'flat-earthers' are still around us and they will want proof that not only a new map is necessary but also they will want to know what was wrong with the old ones. The simple answer is this: our earlier psychological maps were drawn up by well meaning others who thought they knew best. While sometimes that would undoubtedly have been true, the 'best' often ended up by representing what was best *for them*, not me! The crucial need at this point is to claim the right to define ourselves, and not to allow other people to go on doing it for us. The philosopher Kierkegaard said, *"The individual must choose his own identity and not allow himself to be named by the expectations others inflict upon him."* [Quoted in Cox, 1976, p.xvi].

Another powerful reason for drawing up our own 'life-map' is that once we have done that, we are responsible for where it leads us. We take responsibility for our choices, rather than falling back to simply blaming our parents or others in our past for the state of our lives. While we stick to the old maps, we can play the game of 'It's all their fault!' Eric Berne, in his perceptive book *Games People Play* [1964] reveals a whole raft of 'games' people can play in order to avoid taking responsibility for their lives. And this is the decision we must take: we do not fall back to blaming others for the condition of our lives; rather, we stick to the important principle:

What matters most is not what
life throws at us;
But what we *do* with what
life throws at us

So instead of looking backwards, blaming everyone else for how we feel about ourselves – however right some of the blaming may be – we begin to look forwards, we take responsibility for ourselves, and start the process of re-drawing our Life Map based upon a newfound self-esteem.

First, while recognising that the analogy of the old 'mental maps' stands for the traditional way we have inherited from the past our behaviour and attitudinal patterns, we now understand them as transient not permanent. They do not constitute the Law of the Universe, written in stone, but merely the preferences and prejudices of our parents and others.

Secondly, we can consider including on our own psychological map some of those things we were taught were bad. This involves the process called 'deconditioning' – freeing ourselves from our compulsion to feel guilty where no actual guilt exists; and it involves 'reconditioning' ourselves to feel good about things we were never allowed to celebrate.

The prime focus here will be our sexuality.

There is more guilt engendered over sex than any other aspect of our early life. Re-drawing our map will mean an examination of the contents of our childhood 'Sexual Highway Code':

- all the 'no-go' areas on our old maps
- the 'one-way' streets
- the 'no parking' areas
- the Red 'Stop' lights

- the Green 'Go' lights
- the 'No-entry' signs
- Nice boys/girls don't do that!

By the time we reach puberty, many of these instructions are firmly in place. During adolescence most of them get challenged anyway as our hormones change and our bodies prepare for procreation.

At every stage of our revision of sexual attitudes we need to ask these important questions:

- Who taught me that?
- How old was I?
- Where did I learn that?
- Is this still valid?
- Do I still need to be governed by those rules?
- What would I like to see put in its place?

Thirdly, we can exclude all those things that others said *ought* to be done (what psychologists call Introjects), e.g. putting others first, denying ourselves, not upsetting other people, never saying 'no', feeling ashamed, allowing others to walk all over us. We can also include elements which were never allowed to have a look-in: self-acceptance, celebration of who I am and can become, sex without guilt, a good-enough body-image, and the belief that just because I want something does not mean I'm being totally selfish. Harvey Cox says *"it means accepting the terrifying duty of deciding who I will be rather than merely introjecting the stereotypes that others assign to me."* [1976, p.xvi].

Fourth, mapping out a path that we wish to follow. We abandon old, out-worn myths – about God, the universe, others and ourselves. We can create our own story, validate and affirm it. We re-draw most of our personal and spiritual boundaries, including what is beneficial for our own health and excluding what is harmful. Nothing that we have inherited from the past escapes this important review. The old threatening images of God can be destroyed without fear of burning in hell. We can believe that sometimes our parents got it wrong; that others do not have a divine right to love us, nor we them; that we can stop playing games with ourselves and others in order to manipulate the world in the childish way we've always done. Map-making demands that we take responsibility for ourselves; it involves growing up and growing out of out-dated modes of thinking and believing and behaving. It means nothing less than *creating a new world*, finding meaning and value in who we are and in what we do, becoming open to the future instead of terrified by it, and – above all – laying to rest all the ghosts of our past that have hampered and hindered our personal development. Hang on to the wisdom of the words of Paul Tillich:

> *The new comes not out of the old, but out of the death of the old.* [1975, p. 52]

Our personal map will have an in-built flexibility. We can move from those metaphors that implied some kind of predestination for our lives, into a new metaphor that is dynamic and growing and that allows for change.

This new Highway Code is ours – we will neither sell it to, nor inflict it upon, others. Nor will we allow others to change it to suit their needs.

This Highway Code is evidence of our newfound autonomy.

We have fulfilled the most vital task of which Carl Gustav Jung wrote:

> *I asked myself, "What is the myth you are living?" and found that I did not know. So…I took it upon myself to get to know "my" myth, and I regarded this as the task of tasks…I simply had to know what unconscious or preconscious myth was forming me.* [Quoted in, *Your Mythic Journey*, 1989, p. xv]

Breaking free is an important step along the road to self-fulfilment, but it is not enough merely to get outside our personal prison. We must begin to apply our new insights, to use our new maps, and set about re-shaping our future.

CHAPTER SEVEN
Theme: Dance

CELEBRATING OUR NEW STORY

It was a fine feeling that made the spirit of the
Greek Language signify Χρονος, 'formal time',
with a different word from καιρος, 'the right time'...
The consciousness of the καιρος is dependent
on one's being inwardly grasped by the fate
and destiny of the time. Καιρος is every
turning point in history in which the eternal
judges and transforms the temporal.
[Paul Tillich: quoted in
Your Mythic Journey, p.33.]

Χρονος **and** Καιρος

The importance of this distinction in 'time' cannot be over-emphasised. Growth has much more to do with καιρος (kairos) than χρονος (chronos). It is the difference between the 'right moment' and the 'ripe moment'. Many people have asked me during the course of their therapy, "Aren't I too old to change?" My invariable reply was, "Not while you have breath, and the will to change." Indeed, one of my former clients was in her mid-seventies when she came to seek a re-orientation of her life, while others have been in their eighties. Growth has nothing to do with χρονος - how old we are. For many of you, your καιρος has come – the time to grow.

Καιρος is the time of harvest. No farmer harvests his crops because it is the 5th of August or the 8th October. He waits, watches, tests out the degree of humidity with his hydrometer, looks at the weather, consults his instincts, looks up at the sky - then he goes in.

Χρονος time is irrelevant to farmers. They only harvest when the καιρος is right. Dates are not important: the ripeness of the harvest is.

It's like that with human growth of the kind that I have been writing about in this book. We grow at the appropriate time. Some people seem to have to go to hell and back before their time to change is right for them. Therapists – like farmers, yes, and midwives too! – have to learn to be patient and wait upon the unfolding of events. Remember the story of the chrysalis told by Nikos Kazantzakis (p.109)? Premature births can be very risky.

SETTING FORTH

Having come so far, then, in our recognition of all the elements and people that have played a part in our self-development and self-distortion, and discovering that we have a Self waiting to be fulfilled, we have drawn up some new maps – and it is time to set forth on our new journey into the unknown. For many of us it is like being born all over again.

We feel, for example, just as weak and vulnerable as we did

on the day we were born. Questions may flood our minds:

- will I make it?
- will I survive?
- how do I know I'm doing the right thing?
- why do I feel so scared?
- where will it all end?

And there will be mixed feelings too:

- I'm feeling very unsure
- I feel alone
- I feel excited
- It feels scary
- I'm afraid of casting off

Ambivalence will be perhaps our chief awareness – the way we swing to and fro between optimism and pessimism, faith and doubt, strength and weakness, certainty and uncertainty. Naturally, our past history of 'letting go' will surface and we need to recognise what is true of the whole of our journey through life:

That was then – this is now!

I have written about my own experience of 'letting go' elsewhere [1992, chapter 1]. One of the many painful parts of my own leave-taking concerned my decision to take up post-graduate studies in the United States. I was already in a condition of multiple grief, leaving my marriage, my children, my mother, the church – and this all came to a head 35,000 feet above the

Atlantic Ocean on board the 747 Jumbo Jet heading for Boston. I was asked to fill in a Landing Card required by American Immigration. First my name – that was OK. Then, 'Home Address' in the UK. I suddenly burst into tears – wondering what on earth to write since I had no 'home' in the UK. Knowing that would not be good enough for the Immigration Department, and in desperation, I put down my mother's address. I felt absolutely alone. Worse, I now had no base, no roots, no place I could call 'home'. For me, 'setting sail' meant 'jetting off'. I felt truly like a pilgrim, a 'displaced person', and I guess that was what I had chosen to become: a temporary wanderer in search of....what?

To that question I did at least have a few answers. I knew that I had decided upon a new path for myself, constructed a new map, and my studies in America were going to play an important part in my future. I was also searching for healing, for companionship, for a context in which I could continue to grow and where unconditional love might be found. All of this – and so much more – I found within the Chicago Theological Seminary and the people, both staff and students, who helped forward my self-development. But I never forgot that moment on board the 747. Whether the metaphor is 'setting sail' or 'taking off', there is always that moment to negotiate of 'casting off', of 'flight' even. Letting go is going to be hard and possibly painful; but it is absolutely necessary in order to become who we are. I remember there was no one at Heathrow to see me off to Boston, en route for Chicago – and this accentuated the solitariness of my journey. I had said many goodbyes, and although my head was (reasonably) OK about what I was doing, my heart began to tell another part of the story.

As I look back on those moments of my personal journey, I am aware of the tremendous risk that I was taking. I honestly did not know what my future would hold; I had the Siren Voices ringing I my ears, together with enough condemnation and rejection to last me a lifetime. Prophets of doom there were aplenty! But there were also Prophets of hope and joy who supported and encouraged me in going forward in the path that seemed right for me. It felt good to have those around me who believed in me, and in my right to find a new destiny and to take responsibility for my own choices. Although at times I wanted some mothers and fathers to tell me what to do, I only found sisters and brothers that eventually proved far more resourceful. That was part of my growth too – finding others who would allow me to be me without 'mother-smother' love.

NEW LOGOS FOR OLD

It was also time to leave some of my old T-Shirts behind, and decide upon some new ones with different logos. In America, of course, the buyer is spoilt for choice. I particularly liked the T-Shirt Bar where you could choose your own logo from a wide selection of styles and mottoes as well as the chance to make up your own. I bought one with "I survived Chicago!" on the front with my initials, and this seemed appropriate when I was on the point of returning to the UK. (Secretly, I hoped some of my old detractors would take note!)

What would you like to write on the front of your new T-Shirts?

Could you choose a logo that would sum up what you now feel about yourself as opposed to those old logos that others had chosen for you in the past? Your logo may be in words, but perhaps it could be a symbol or picture that summarises your new believe in your Self? Many people have begun to draw again, not for assessment by others, as in our 'Art Class' at school, but purely for the joy of experimenting with another side of our self-expression. Creating our own Logo or Symbol might be a way of summing-up the new emerging Self. Others have turned to writing poetry. My own Logo was that of a butterfly. Perhaps you will need several pictures or symbols unless you are lucky enough to find one that includes the whole of your story.

Your story – ah! yes, that's going to be important, too.

FINDING, OWNING AND TELLING YOUR OWN STORY

This is where Carl Jung's quotation, with which the last chapter ended, has important relevance. "What is the myth you are living?" I find Sam Keen's description of 'myth' both illuminating and encouraging:

> *Myth is the software, the cultural DNA, the unconscious information, the metaprogram that governs the way we see 'reality' and the way we behave.*
>
> *...the entire legacy and burden of cultural and family myth comes to rest on the individual. Each person is a repository of stories. To the degree that any one of us reaches towards autonomy, we must begin a process of sorting through the trash and treasures we have been given, keeping some and rejecting others. We gain the full dignity and power of our persons only when we create a narrative account of our lives, dramatize our existence, and forge a coherent personal myth that combines elements of our cultural myth and family myth with*

> *unique stories that come from our experience.* [1989, pp.xii and xiv]

In many ways, I have been sharing my own myth with you as we have journeyed together through the pages of this book. My myth is mine, not yours. I share it only for information, encouragement and education, not because this is **the** way. It happens to be my way; you will have to write your own myth. But there is a lot to be gained by reading how it is and has been for others, and by implication how it could be for you. It may be useful to provide an outline of how to write a personal myth. Much will be found that is valuable and informative in the book by Sam Keen and Anne Valley-Fox that I have quoted above, but here is a summary for you to consider:

The Question	**The Issue**
Where did I come from?	[Origins]
Who were my earliest teachers about life?	[Models]
How close should I get to people?	[Boundaries]
What is good and what is bad?	[Ethics]
What do I believe about my world?	[Cosmology]
What is ugly or beautiful?	[Aesthetics]
Where am I going?	[Destiny]
With whom do I belong?	[Intimacy]
What happens when I die?	[Religion]
How do I understand what love is?	[Spirituality]

The list is only an example to get you started, but like all adventures you always find other things and other issues confronting you as your Journey proceeds. Indeed, this is part of the excitement and challenge. It may look like hard work, but in the end we will find that we really have no choice. Once our old world, defined by our old map, is found to be obsolete, we simply have to draw a new one. This is what all the ancient discoverers, especially the pioneer seamen like Columbus, had to do. They simply found that the older maps, worthwhile and useful perhaps in their time, were not only obsolete but also dangerous.

A New World demanded new maps!

While the questions above are only tentative ones, they are there to help you focus on the whole of you – your belief systems especially – since these govern the way we think and the way we behave. As we begin to let go of the old atlas of our past, we may feel a pang of disloyalty to those who gave it to us. They were not, by any means, all bad people or intended us harm. On the contrary, many of them were merely handing on to us what had been given to them, and there might well be much wisdom in this tradition handed down to us that is of permanent validity and usefulness. But sorting out the wheat from the chaff is the task of every person who is beginning to take responsibility for his or her own life. No longer can we blame others for giving us maps that we now find to be out-of-date; many of those people were undoubtedly sincere. Some might even have revised the maps handed down to them; others would simply have passed them on un-revised. Whatever we received, however, it is now up to us to do something about it, rather than simply blame others for our past. How can we deal with this in a practical manner?

DEALING WITH OUR PAST

There are several ways in which we may view our past, especially our earliest childhood experiences, and I will outline the choices we seem to have:

1. **The Way of Blindness**: Nothing is changed; past repeated.
2. **The Way of Blame**: We blame other people; resentment.
3. **The Way of Change**: We take responsibility for ourselves.

In the First Way, we have no idea about how we were shaped by our earliest influences in the home, school and family relationships. We are in a state of unawareness, and plenty of people wish to stay that way. They do not wish to know, and probably think that people who begin contemplating their existential navel have something wrong with them. They're OK the way they are, thank you very much! Of course, very often this is not a choice at all, merely the continuation of "as it was in the beginning, is now, and ever shall be…"

In the Second Way, a certain awareness has begun to take place, enough for them to realise something of what went on in their past, perhaps discovered as a result of reading, counselling or therapy. Light begins to dawn that there are reasons why they are the way they are, and early pain and emotional deprivation may well be recalled. But there they stay, resentful of their past and of the people who were responsible for their own damage. They appear to rest content with having a scapegoat, someone to blame for all their ills. Their cry is, "Well, what can you expect of a person who had an alcoholic mother/abusive father/adopted parents?" or whatever. It is what

Eric Berne calls *The Wooden Leg Game*. This type of behaviour is one that justifies personal pathology as the fault of other people. No responsibility is taken at all for personal behaviour; it is all the fault of others 'who made me this way'. (I have written elsewhere about this syndrome and you may care to look further at my *Don't Blame Me!* [1990]). In this Second stage, people are perhaps the most miserable of all, since there is enough insight to know how they came to be the way they are, but have little or no desire for change. Personal therapy can help, but eventually the way out is to move on to our third stage.

In this Third Way, we move into the Way of Change. It is important at this point to realise that there is no way in which we can change anything of our past personal history.

What happened in the past cannot be changed.

We must abandon - if indeed we ever entertained – the idea that somehow we can change our past, have the perfect childhood and perfect parents that we never had, and get all our physical, spiritual and emotional needs met that never were met in our past.

This is simply a pipe dream.

It is an understandable one, with which many people enter into counselling or psychotherapy, but nevertheless a mistaken one. There is simply nothing that either we or others can do to give us the good we lacked in our childhood, or take away the bad that happened to us in the past. As Edward Fitzgerald wrote:

The Moving finger writes, and, having writ,

> *moves on: nor all thy piety nor wit*
> *Shall lure it back to cancel half a line,*
> *nor all thy tears wash out a word of it.*
> [*The Rubaiyat of Omar Khayyam,* 1859, Stanza 51]

For most of us, this is the worst possible news that we can ever receive. And yet, as we come to think about it a little more, we see that this is inevitable. None of us can turn the clocks back and make a new start. The only place to make a new start is from where we find ourselves at the present.

The issue in this Third Way is succinctly put by Dorothy Rowe:

> *...what matters most is not what our parents did to us but what we do with what our parents did to us.* [1983, p.161]

As I stated earlier, in my more generalised version of Rowe's words, we could expand this important insight and make it even more global:

> *What matters most is not what life has thrown at us, but what we are doing with what life has thrown at us.*

It is an insight as old as the first century AD when the famous Greek philosopher Epictetus wrote, *"Men are disturbed not by things but by the views which they take of them."* In other words, the task of those of us who want to change is not to think about changing the past, but to change the way we *react* to what has occurred in our past. It is time to take responsibility for dealing more creatively and effectively with what the past has dealt out to us.

For instance, if 'what our parents did to us' was to give us an inferiority complex by putting us down and robbing us of our self-esteem, we can begin by challenging (inside ourselves) this whole idea. If 'what our parents did to us' was to create a chronic dependency upon grown-ups and eroded our own worth and power, we can begin by discovering within ourselves the power and ability that we were never able to discover when we were young. This is at the extreme end of how we have habitually regarded ourselves, but instead of continuing to believe that our parents were right – or to blame them for being wrong – we now take responsibility for how we are going to react in the here and now. A particularly pertinent example of how this might work out is given in Frances Hodgson Burnett's book, *The Secret Garden*, and Agnieska Holland's beautiful film based on it.

The story concerns a little girl, Mary Lennox, who is orphaned while living with her parents in India. She eventually comes back to England to live with her mother's brother, and his formidable housekeeper, Mrs. Medlock. The house is large and rambling and in her boredom Mary begins to explore the house and gardens. Curious about some strange crying, Mary discovers a young boy incarcerated in a large room. The windows are boarded up and only a small nightlight lights the room. Within this dingy atmosphere the boy ekes out his pitiful shadow of a life. He is in fact the cousin of Mary, her uncle's son, Colin. Here is the significant moment when Mary and Colin meet for the first time.

C: *Tell me your name again.*
M: *Mary Lennox. Did no one ever tell you I had to come to live here?*
C: *No…they daren't.*

M: *Why?*
C: *Because I should have been afraid you would see me. I won't let people see me and talk me over.*
M: *Why?*
C: *Because I am like this always, ill and having to lie down. My father won't let people talk me over either. The servants are not allowed to speak about me. If I live I may be a hunchback, but I shan't live. My father hates to think I may be like him.*

Later on, a sinister fact is introduced innocently by Colin that helps us to understand the deeper significance of what is happening to him:

C: *I don't suppose that I shall live. Ever since I can remember anything I have heard people say I shan't. At first they thought I was too little to understand and now they think I don't hear. My doctor is my father's cousin. He is quite poor and if I die he will have all Misslthwaite [Manor] when my father is dead. I should think he wouldn't want me to live.*
M: *Do you want to live?*
C: *No, but I don't want to die.*

From the point of view of our present interest, what Frances Hodgson Burnett has given to us is the story of the systematic destruction of a young life. Here is evil in demonstrable form. The Lion, the Witch and the Wardrobe are here for all to see in their manifest wickedness. Colin is being sacrificed on the altar of his doctor's avarice and his father's inability to cope with his wife's death. Since the boy reminds him too much of his late wife, he must be banished. More than that, he must be 'pathologised' (to coin a phrase) in order to give the family a cover story for his separation and isolation. All of the family's pathology is projected onto the small child, making him an *invalid* (= without value). With that weight placed upon him, no wonder he feels like a hunchback. He is made to bear his father's denial of grief, and to be banished from his presence merely because he reminds his father too much of his late wife. The cover story is that he 'does not want to see people'; the truth is the opposite. He must be concealed and hidden away and must not be seen. (Here is an example of what we called earlier, Reaction Formation.) Eventually, as we see in the conversation above, Colin himself colludes with this story, by wishing to remain concealed. The death-wish planted on him by his father, now becomes Colin's own, with the glorious exception of that last ambiguous reply to Mary's question as to whether he wants to live. *"No, but I don't want to die."* The spark of life is left alive within Colin, despite what his parent and his minions have wrought upon him.

How the story develops you must find out for yourselves by reading the book or, better still, see the beautifully filmed version, but there is a strong therapeutic (indeed, redemptive) theme running right through. It is the story of how a young child can be 'pathologised' and turned into a permanent invalid, losing almost every wish to live, and how even he can be brought back to life again. What mattered most to Colin in the end was not what his parenting had done to him but what he was going to do with what his parenting had done to him. He took responsibility for his own life and went on a journey of self-discovery. He chose the Way of Change. He found life.

Examples such as these abound in literature. It is a common human theme running through the classics – so we know that the issue is far from a modern one, and one that certainly does not owe its discovery to the psychotherapeutic revolution of the second half of the twentieth century. What that revolution has, however, contributed to our understanding are the theoretical and psychological tools whereby such early childhood damage can be uncovered, understood, believed and remedied. People who tell stories such as Colin's have begun to revise their old life maps and dared to move out into a far more glorious future than they could ever have dreamed about. It is not insignificant that one of the last glimpses we get of Colin is that of dancing in the secret garden.

THE METAPHOR OF DANCE

Among the many familiar metaphors of fulfilment of our lives is that of the dance. In his unforgettable novel, *Zorba the Greek*, Nikos Kazantzakis makes the dance the focal symbol of his hero's attitude to life, as distinguished from that of 'the Boss' who lives life on a very tight, well-controlled rein, goose-stepping through life. The story is about these two very different characters – in birth, background and behaviour – and how Boss gradually comes to appreciate the freedom and liberty that characterises Zorba's life. The most moving scene comes one night on the beach when the Boss simply says to Zorba,

> *"Teach me to dance!"*
> *"Zorba leaped to his feet, his face sparkling.*
> *'To dance, boss? To dance? Fine! Come on!'*
> *'Off we go, then, Zorba! My life has changed! Let's have it!'"*

As Sam Keen reflects [1971, p.160] –

> ***Perhaps Zorba is the saint for our time***

The dance is a universal symbol. It can include prescribed steps and it can be as free as we care to make it. It can involve touch and closeness as well as separation and distance. It can be experienced with many others, with one other or by oneself. It can be both measured and spontaneous. As Sam Keen explains:

> *Authentic love is a dance with three movements: solo, counterpoint, and coming together; it embraces solitude, conflict, and intimacy. Leave any one of three movements out and you destroy the dance.* [1991, p.190]

I remember one evening on the island of Rhodes, visiting the small Taverna just near the hotel where I was staying. Periodically, with no apparent invitation or arrangement, various people would get up and dance to the accompaniment of a small group of instrumentalists, while I sipped my cool beer wondering if I could ever find the courage to get up and dance. Suddenly, Zorba's tune started up very slowly and invitingly, and one young local Greek man got up and started to dance on his own. At first, it was like a solo performance and no one dared to interrupt it, but my feet grew itchy and I could no longer deny my need to share in this young man's dance. I joined him on the floor, feeling very stupid and self-conscious. At first, there was no eye contact between us, and then suddenly I found myself caught up in the extrovert music of Mikis Theodorakis, the power of which seemed to resonate with energy surging within my body. Slowly, I circled round and eventually, we seemed to come to a point when our steps were in total syncopation. We seemed to know each other's moves before we made them, and then we smiled when it worked. The music grew louder and faster and we encircled the floor, and one another, oblivious to the crowd of people in the Taverna who were now beating time with their hands. It seemed at that moment that we were somehow creating the music instead of responding to it. The music inside and outside came to a climax and we finished together, breathless. Not a word was exchanged but I fancied a wry smile on the young Greek's face, which I interpreted as, "An Englishman! And he dances!" The applause was deafening, and I returned to my seat for several more beers to cool off. It seemed that in a magical moment, my new life was being affirmed, and that somehow – in the intimacy of the dance – I was making a statement to myself about my new-found freedom and identity.

Each of us has a dance within us – not perhaps in any conventional sense, and certainly not involving learning steps or going to dancing classes. It has to come from within us. It seems that we and the dance are one. And one writer gives us the hope that the dance will go on even after our physical life comes to an end. Sydney Carter wrote his familiar song, *Lord of the Dance* in 1967, in which he espouses the idea that God is the Lord of the Dance of life which death itself cannot overcome or interrupt.

Finally, the poet Kahlil Gibran, gives expression to this hope that there is something eternal in life as the dance. He wrote words that could become a hope springing up within all of us:

> *For what is it to die but to stand naked in the wind and to melt into the sun?*
> *And what is it to cease breathing but to free the breath from its restless tides, that it may rise and expand and seek God unencumbered?*
> *Only when you drink from the river of silence shall you indeed sing.*

And when you have reached the mountain top, then you shall begin to climb.
And when the earth shall claim your limbs, then shall you truly dance.
[1976, p. 94.]

EPILOGUE

Of all the people in classical literature from whom I take courage is Odysseus - the archetypal Hero. In the Classics, the Hero is the traveller, the one who sets out on a journey, frequently perilous and always into the unknown.

Odysseus was the Greek hero returning from the Trojan War, and a journey that should have taken him three weeks turned into a ten-year epic. For him, this returning home to Ithaca turned into a journey of personal transformation.

You, too, since you have come this far, have been reminded again and again of the risks involved in the journey of becoming who you are. I have not hesitated to share with you part of my own journey since I know how much I owe to those people who had the courage to share the pain and hopes of their journey with me. In the depths of my own doubts and anxieties about my future, it was encouraging to read how other pilgrims had negotiated their journeys and eventually reached 'home'. At one point, I had almost given up hope of even physically surviving my various ordeals. Ironically, it was a book that gave me the courage to continue my quest for a new life.

That book was Robert Raines' *Going Home.* I was in my room at the Chicago Theological Seminary when one of the other doctoral students breezed in and tossed a book onto my bed, saying it might be of interest. I had already shared with him part of my story, and as I opened the book I soon discovered that it was like reading *my own diary*!

Raines' story was a complete parallel to my own: the

checklist was quite uncanny. He was leaving a marriage of over 20 years (check); leaving behind his four children (check) and parents (check); leaving his church ministry after 20 years (check); and leaving behind a concept of God that no longer worked for him (check). The effect upon me was quite electric: but quite apart from the similarities of our situations, what struck me most as I devoured his story, was that he eventually succeeded in surviving the journey, and emerged into a new and more wholesome life.

I recall sobbing my heart out, and saying out loud, "Thank God; he survived!"

And it was true in my own experience that I, too, "survived Chicago". So I am under no illusions concerning the dangers and heart-aches that are part and parcel of every heroic journey into personal transformation. It comes down in the end to trusting the process, and being drawn not so much to answers as being drawn by the questions. I have little doubt that you have found your own list of questions as you negotiated this book. If you have found a new way to self-acceptance, and an end to inherited patterns of self-rejection, you may well resonate to, and rejoice in, the words of Robert Raines:

> *I could hear that distant drumbeat sound within, and it was time to obey it, follow it, step to it, learn its rhythm and cadence, and discover it as my authentic dance, even if it meant stepping outside the drill team line-up.* [p.42]

That 'drumbeat sound within' is always the experience of the Hero/ine who dares to question the *status quo*, and sets out to find a new self-concept and a new way of living. Like Odysseus, we too will experience one distraction after another (remember the Sirens?), and the Ibsen-like 'Torvalds' who question both our morality and even our sanity and, when that fails, they try the time-honoured way of inducing guilt. Resist them all.

"Don't let the world around you squeeze you into its own mould..." (St. Paul).

It's time for you to discover, own and celebrate who you are – time to leave the cocoon of the past – and fly!

The seed that is to grow
Must lose itself as seed;
And they that creep
May graduate through
Chrysalis to wings.
Wilt thou then, O mortal,
Cling to husks which
Falsely seem to you
The self?
[Wu Ming Fu, Chinese poet, philosopher.
Patterns in Jade.]

Shalom!

ACKNOWLEDGEMENTS

This book would not have been possible without the assistance and inspiration of a variety of people and sources I have been fortunate to have met.

In no particular order of importance I must express my thanks:

To the late Dr. Frank Lake and my friends and former colleagues in the Clinical Theology Association, and in particular Alison Hunter, and the late Ted Kettell and Ron Files for their patience and expertise;

To my mentors and colleagues with the American Association for Clinical Pastoral Education at The University of Chicago Medical Clinics;

To my Clinical supervisors, Drs. David Toms and Judith Anderson, for their support and encouragement, and their loving exposure of my own shortcomings in the practice and theory of psychotherapy;

To Dr. Steve Reno for his support in the darker moments of the journey into my psychological interior; for introducing me to the wealth of Sam Keen, Nikos Kazantzakis, Laurence Durrell and Californian wines;

To Michael Jacobs for his encouragement and acceptance into a collegiality from which I derived much knowledge and not a little pleasure;

To my former students in Leicester University and St. John's College, Nottingham, from whom I learned so much about the process of personal change, for challenging some of my assumptions and the practice of psychotherapy;

To Professors Phil Anderson and Bob Moore, and the students in the class of '81 at the Chicago Theological Seminary; for their acceptance, their unconditional love and for teaching me how to love and to celebrate myself;

To the many pioneers in the Human Potential movement from whom I have gained so much; for all that they inspired within me and for providing me with creative models of existence – especially Eric Berne, Fritz Perls, John Rowan and Sheldon Kopp;

To my daughter, Gill Howard, for her loving support and for reading an early draft and making valuable comments;

To Philip Dodd for his help with the illustration on p62;

To Dr. Sophie Hadfield-Hill for the cover photograph;

To my wife Jan, for helping to keep my theory and my practice more congruent than they might otherwise have been; for her love and support, my deepest thanks.

BIBLIOGRAPHY

Baum, L. F. (1900) *The Wizard of Oz.*

Bennett, A. (1994) *Writing Home*, Faber & Faber.

Berne, E. (1964) *Games People Play*, Penguin.

Bridges, W. (1980) *Transitions*, Addison-Wesley.

Burnett, F. H. (1911) *The Secret Garden.*

Cardinal, M. (1984) *The Words to Say It*, Picador.

Cox, H. (1969) *The Feast of Fools*, Harvard University Press.

Cox, H. (1976) *On Not Leaving It To The Snake*, Macmillan.

Freud, S. (1961) *The Future of an Illusion* (ed. James Strachey) Norton.

Fromm, E. (1975) *The Art of Loving*, Unwin.

Forward, S. (1989) *Toxic Parents*, Bantam Books.

Gibran, K. (1976) *The Prophet*, Heinemann.

Gough, T. (1990) *Don't Blame Me!*, DLT.

Gough, T. (1992) *Couples Parting*, DLT.

Gough, T. (1994) *Therapeutic Perspectives in the Adventures of Mr. Toad:* Journal of the British Association for Counselling, Vol. 5, No. 4.

Grof, S. (1975) *The Realms of the Human Unconscious*, Viking Press.

Hafner, J. (1993) *The End of Marriage*, Century.

Harris, T. (1970) *I'm OK, You're OK.* Pan.

Jacobs, M. (1986) *The Presenting Past*, Harper & Row.

Janov, A. (1970) *The Primal Scream*, Abacus.

Janov, A. (1975) *Primal Man: The New Consciousness*, Abacus.

Kazantzakis, N. (1973) *Report to Greco*, Faber & Faber.

Keen, S. (1970) *To A Dancing God*, Fontana.

Keen, S. (1975) *Beginnings without End*, Harper & Row.
Keen, S. & Valley-Fox, A. (1989) *Your Mythic Journey*, Jeremy P. Tarcher.
Keen, S. (1991) *Fire in the Belly*, Bantam.
Keen, S. (1994) *Hymns to the Unknown God*, Jeremy P. Tarcher.
Kopp, S. (1979) *If You Meet The Buddha On The Road, Kill Him!* Sheldon.
Kopp, S. (1987) *Who Am I…Really?* Jeremy P. Tarcher.
Laing, R. D. (1965) *The Divided Self*, Penguin.
Laing, R. D. (1976) *The Facts of Life*, Penguin.
Lake, F. (1981) *Tight Corners in Pastoral Counselling*, DLT.
Lake, F. (1986) *Clinical Theology*, (Abridged Version) DLT.
Leboyer, F. (1979) *Birth Without Violence*, Fontana.
Levinson, D.J. (1978) *The Seasons of a Man's Life*, Ballantine Books.
Lewis, C. S. (1950) *The Lion, the Witch & The Wardrobe*, Puffin.
Lowen, A. (1985) *Narcissism: Denial of the True Self*, Collier.
Nelson-Jones, R.(1983) *Practical Counselling Skills*, Rinehart & Winston.
Noble, E. (1993) *Primal Connections*, Fireside.
Odent, M. (1984) *Entering the World*, Penguin.
Peck, M. S. (1983) *People of the Lie*, Rider.
Peters, J. (1989) *Frank Lake: The Man and His Work*, DLT.
Proto, L. (1985) *Self-Healing*, Piatkus.
Rank, O. (1975) *The Realms of the Human Unconscious*, Viking Press.
Rank, O. (1924) *The Trauma of Birth*, Warner Torch Books.
Raines, R. (1979) *Going Home*, Harper & Row.
Rayner, E. (1986) *Human Development*, Unwin Hyman.
Rieu, E. V. (1980) *The Illustrated Odyssey*, Sidgwick & Jackson.
Rowan, J. (1983) *The Reality Game*, RKP.
Rowan, J. (1990) *Subpersonalities*, RKP.

Rowe, D. (1983) *Depression: The Way out of your Prison*, RKP.
Russell, W. (1989) *Shirley Valentine*, Methuen.
Schultz, W. (1979) *Profound Simplicity*, Turnstone Books.
Schreiber, F. R. (1973) *Sybil*, Penguin.
Schwartz, L. (1980) *The World of the Unborn Child*, Richard Marek.
Thorne, B. (1992) *Carl Rogers*, Sage.
Verny, T. (1982) *The Secret Life of the Unborn Child*, Sphere.
Weldon, F. (1980) *Puffball*, Coronet Books.
Wilber, K. (1985) *No Boundary: Eastern & Western Approaches to Personal Growth*, New Science Library.
Zinker, J. (1977) *The Creative Process in Gestalt Therapy*, NY, Vintage.

INDEX